B. Chirva

SOCCER
Gaming drills with the contiguous goals for play technique training

2016

УДК 796 332
Ч 64

Ч 64 **Chirva B.** Soccer. Gaming drills with the contiguous goals for play technique training. – 2016. – 122 с.

ISBN 978-5-98724-189-9

In this book the principles, the method and the methodical techniques of build-up of gaming drills with the contiguous goals for play technique training by the players are described.

More than 50 gaming drills with the contiguous goals, focused on training of attacking and defending actions training in 18-yard box, zone of attack and midfield zone, are listed.

УДК 796 332
Ч 64

ISBN 978-5-98724-189-9

© Chirva B., «ТВТ Дивизион», 2016

All rights reserved

CONTENTS

INTRODUCTION... 6
THE SYMBOLS... 8

CHAPTER I. CONCEPT DESCRIPTION OF GAMING DRILLS WITH THE CONTIGUOUS GOALS FOR PLAY TECHNIQUE TRAINING.. 10
1. 1. Principles of drills build-up............................... 10
1. 2. Method and methodical techniques of drills build-up..10
1. 3. Drills classification..14

CHAPTER II. GAMING DRILLS WITH THE CONTIGOUOS GOALS FOR PLAY TECHNIQUE TRAINING IN THE 18-YARD BOX..16
2. 1. Drills elaboration...16
2. 2. Drills examples...21
Section 1. Drills implying only individual actions......................................21
Section 2. Drills implying shots on goal by the leg in the crowded conditions.........................23
Section 3. Drills implying shots on goal by the leg having used the first touch.........................29
Section 4. Drills implying obligatory movements with the ball..32
Section 5. Drills implying timely passes for shots on goal..34
Section 6. Drills implying shots on goal and passes by the head..46

CHAPTER III. GAMING DRILLS WITH THE CONTIGOUOS GOALS FOR PLAY TECHNIQUE TRAINING IN THE ZONE OF ATTACK.................................. 52
3. 1. Drills elaboration... 52
3. 2. Drills examples..58
Section 1. Drills implying shots on goal from the outside of the 18-yard box........................... 58
Section 2. Drills implying delivery of the ball in the 18-yard box having used a pass................. 69
Section 3. Drills implying delivery of the ball in the 18-yard box having used dribbling............... 78
Section 4. Drills implying delivery of the ball in the 18-yard box having used dribbling or a pass depending on situation.................. 86

CHAPTER IV. GAMING DRILLS WITH THE CONTIGOUOS GOALS FOR PLAY TECHNIQUE TRAINING IN THE MIDFIELD ZONE................................100
4. 1. Drills elaboration...100
4. 2. Drills examples..102
Section 1. Drills implying space overcoming having used combination of dribbling and passing of the ball on short and mean distances.........102
Section 2. Drills implying space overcoming having used passing by the second touch, executed after the first without delay........................108
Section 3. Drills implying space overcoming having used passing on a mean and long distances..112

CHAPTER V. THE FEATURES OF GAMING DRILLS BUILD-UP WITH THE CONTIGUOUS GOALS IN THE COURSE OF PLAY TECHNIQUE TRAINING OF YOUNG PLAYERS........................ 116

CONCLUSION... 118
BIBLIOGRAPHY... 120

SOCCER. Gaming drills with the contiguous goals for play technique training

INTRODUCTION

During the competitive games players can act deliberately (if know what to do in advance) and off hand, when they are to choose and execute one of several potential actions.

If players possess the high «deliberate actions with the ball» technique, that doesn't mean yet they can successfully act in situations when it's necessary to take a right decision from many possible and accomplish it. That's exactly why the training of «deliberate actions with the ball» technique assumes paramount importance.

At the present day there are three kinds of exercises for techniques building-up, which excel in that during players act with the ball:
– actions begin and end conventionally;
– actions begin conventionally and end variatively;
– actions begin and end variatively.

The conditions of drills with variative beginning and variative ending of actions of players with the ball provide footballers with the possibilities to act impromptu and exercise technically different methods of performance of skills depending on situation.

One of the types of drills with variative beginning and variative ending of players actions with the ball is the gaming drills with the contiguous goals of regular size, which are defended by goalkeepers, small amount of players in field and specific restrictions and objectives.

These drills meet the requirements of competitive matches to the greatest extent and allow highly qualified players to improve the mastery of attacking and defending actions, while younger footballers to acquire the technique of these actions.

Goalkeepers participating in gaming drills with the contiguous goals get the opportunity to train a lot of time in the most favorable conditions to develop the most important for them anticipation reactions: anticipation of process of game situations and moment, speed and direction of the ball towards the goal depending on player movements.

This book gives a general characteristic of gaming drills with the contiguous goals and their classification according to the predominant focus in training specific attacking and defensive actions in different areas of the field.

Provides the examples of these drills for training of play technique in 18-yard box, attacking zone and midfield with the indication of parameters of task construction and requirements for players and goalkeepers actions (playing area size, number of players, target settings for footballers, restrictions for certain actions, playing time in one repeat etc.).

A separate section discusses the features of gaming exercises with contiguous goals for the purpose of training techniques play in preparing young players.

THE SYMBOLS

In characteristic of footballers actions in competitive play and description of gaming exercises with the contiguous gates in this book will use the symbols shown in the fig. 1.

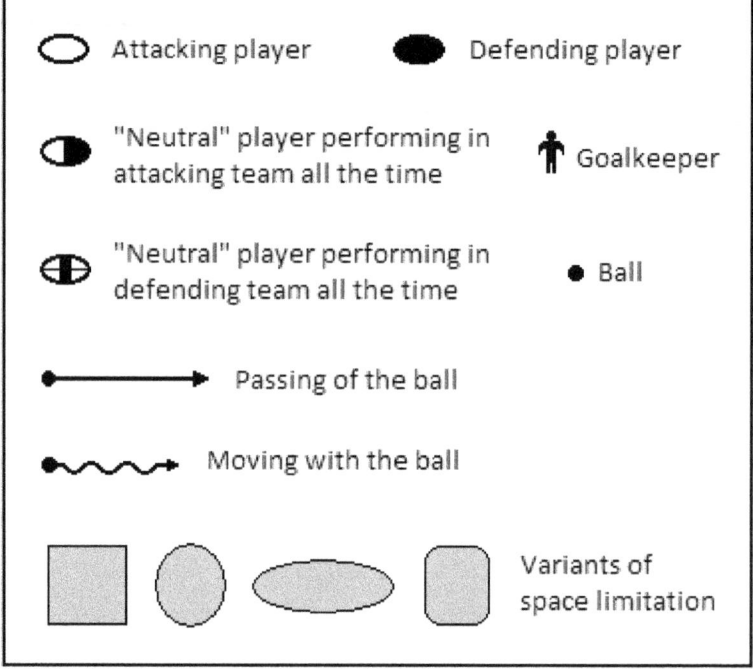

Fig. 1. The symbols that will be used for characteristic of footballers actions in competitive games and description of gaming exercises with the contiguous goals

SOCCER. Gaming drills with the contiguous goals for play technique training

For notes

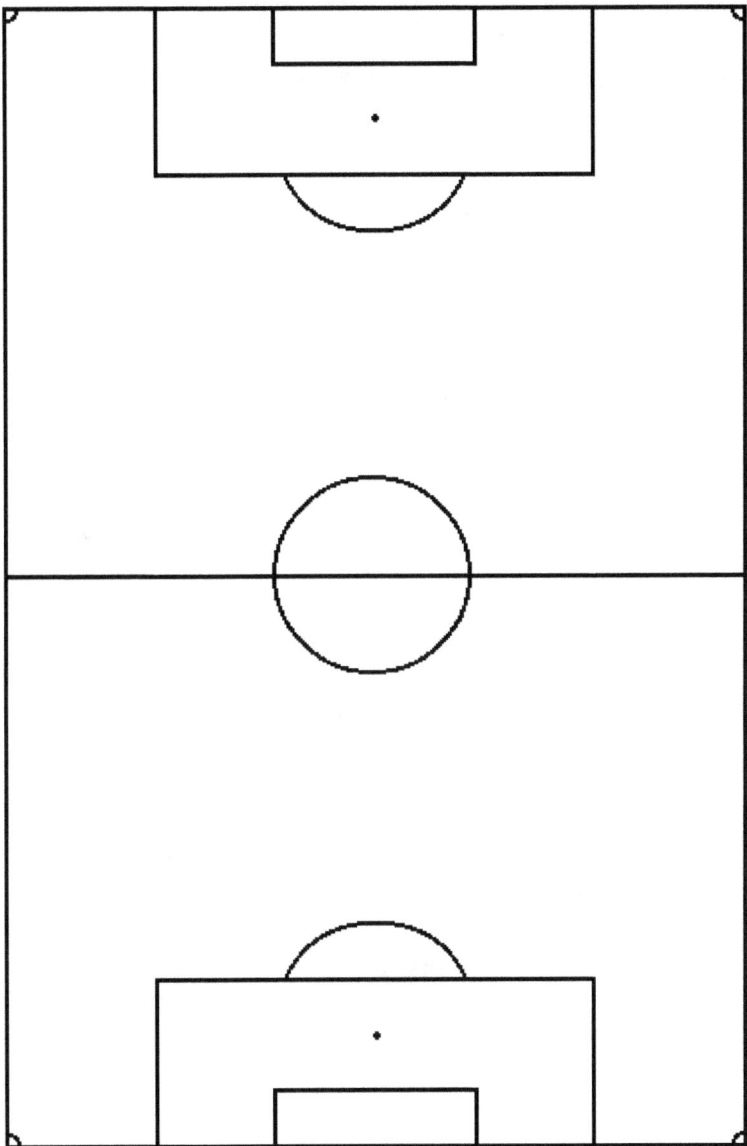

CHAPTER 1. CONCEPT DESCRIPTION OF GAMING DRILLS WITH THE CONTIGUOUS GOALS FOR PLAY TECHNIQUE TRAINING

1. 1. Principles of drills build-up

There is a specific technique of actions with the ball («game episodes technique») that corresponds with definite football episodes. Hence gaming drills with the contiguous goals are based on the observance of two general principles:
– development of special conditions on technique of actions with the ball performance in competitive games in specific areas of the pitch and of those requirements that apply to the players on the display of precision and speed of actions of the ball in these areas;
– providing possibilities for every player to perform large amount of actions with the ball repetition in these conditions.

1. 2. Method and methodical techniques of drills build-up

Realization of general principles of gaming drills with the contiguous goals build-up presupposes the following general method of its organization: conduction of the game on the small size pitch with two goals of standard size protected by the goalkeepers, and small number of players in teams.
All players taking part in these exercises (both goalkeepers and players in field) should perform with maximum responsibility and commitment.

Using definite methodical procedures in the process of organization of exercises «game with the contiguous goals» allow to provide conditions for training not only attacking and defending actions technique, but a wide range of individual and group tactical actions either.

In addition physical activity come to footballers may be scheduled sufficiently enough, for the purpose of their functional capabilities improvement.

Following methodical procedures may be applied.

1. Change of size and configuration of playing ground, mounting position of a goal.

Variation of playing ground size allows to provide players density on definite areas and thus to simulate episodes of scoring in competitive games in the context of space deficit.

Change of configuration of playing ground inspires players to use one or another manner of delivery of the ball to shooting position. For example, on short and wide playing ground players get more opportunities for crosses (from the flank) (fig. 2a), while on narrow and long – for moving with the ball with crossing of sufficiently large space (fig. 2b).

Mounting of the goals in such a manner that they aren't situated opposite but dislocated relative to each other down the goal line (fig. 2c) allows to increase number of shots at goal from the position at an angle to it from a longer distance and accomplish passes on longer distances.

2. Variation of number of players participating in drill.

Optimum number of players participating in gaming drills with the contiguous goals (if there's a task to develop actions with the ball technique in particular) is from one to four in each team.

It's problematical to achieve large amount of actions with the ball repetition by every player with the bigger number of players.

There may be introduced «neutral» players in exercises who play for attacking or defending team constantly. Whereby, respectively, conditions of execution of attacking actions by footballers are facilitated or hampered.

Changing the number of drill participants and simultaneously the size of playing ground we can regulate overcrowding of players in definite space, frequency of players contacts with the ball, physical activity of players, and also perfect different tactical interactions.

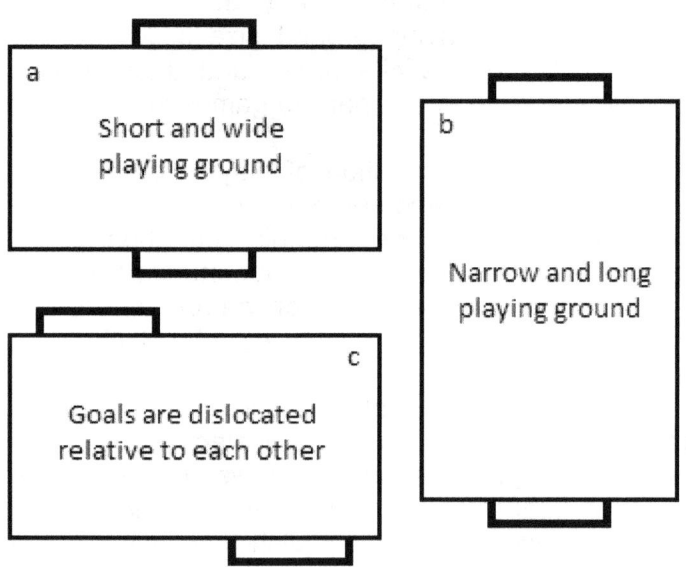

Fig. 2. Examples of playing ground configuration and mounting of goals while building-up of gaming drills with the contiguous goals

3. Encourage players to perform definite actions by way of stimulation of various kinds.

The extent of one or another player actions with the ball can be increased by way of stimulation of a player or a team for performance of these actions.

For example, drill conditions may involve shots on goal by both foot and head, but to encourage performance of headers exactly, any header towards goal can be considered as a goal, and a goal scored by head – as three goals.

To stimulate the players to finish off the ball into the net goal scored in such manner may count as two.

4. Restrictions on any actions with the ball.

Restrictions on the performance of definite actions with the ball allow increasing the amount of repetitions of exactly those techniques and technical elements, training of which is the main purpose of the drill. It may be imposed on:

– number of passes from one player to another in one team, performance of passes from players to goalkeeper, time of possession, that allows to increase the number of shots on goal;

– putting the ball into play by goalkeepers in any way, executing of attacking actions by players through definite area of playing ground or in a certain way;

– number of touches of the ball by each player that allows to regulate the amount of individual actions with the ball, for example, restriction on play in one or two touches impels players to act with the ball and move with the ball quickly.

5. Observation of certain football rules.

Depending on object in view in drills «play with the contiguous goals» certain football rules, such as offside, corners, throwing the ball from the sideline, may be observed or not.

6. Use of reserve ball.

To increase the amount of players actions with the ball and vary the intensity of tasks performance there can be used definite number of reserve balls that originally fit into one or another goal and introduced into the game by the goalkeepers, when «game» ball leaves drill area far-off.

For example availability of 8 reserve balls (4 in each goal) during the performance of «one on one» game within 1 minute of play almost always provides maximum intensity of players actions.

1. 3. Drills classification

There are three stages that can be marked in any attack finishing with the shot on goal: beginning, evolvement and finishing. Therefore game episodes during which players pretend to score a goal may be grouped on common attributes depending on:
— how they begin (from the ball takeover by players during the game after a partner's pass and as a result of charge or interception of the ball from the opponent or after putting the ball into play from the set pieces);
— where they begin and evolve;
— where they finish.

Players decisions about actions with the ball and technical performance of techniques on every stage of attack in competitive games are taken with some aspects that are defined by the circumstances and place of actions with the ball.

As a result the same characteristic features of players decisions about actions with the ball and technical performance of techniques on different sections of the pitch must be involved in gaming drills with the contiguous goals either.

There are three kinds of «game episodes technique» defined on the ground of analysis of terms and particular characteristics of performance of actions with the ball by the players: in 18-yard box, attacking zone (no further than 35 meters from the goal line of defending team) and middle section of the pitch (no closer than 35 meters from the goal line of defending team).

Consequently there are three groups of gaming drills with the contiguous goals for training of «game episodes technique»:

– in 18-yard box;
– in attacking zone;
– in middle section of the pitch.

Different game situations in competitive games differ in amount of contribution of players successful actions in these situations to the outcome of definite match. This essentially defines what should be paid more attention and devotes more time in training.

Considering the critical importance of players mastery in performance of attacking and defending actions un 18-yard box and attacking zone for achieving victory in game the most attention in this book will be paid to gaming drills with the contiguous goals focused on perfection of play technique in 18-yard box and attacking zone.

CHAPTER II.
GAMING DRILLS WITH THE CONTIGOUOS GOALS FOR PLAY TECHNIQUE TRAINING IN THE 18-YARD BOX

2. 1. Drills elaboration

During the elaboration of gaming drills with the contiguous goals for play technique training in 18-yard box several provisions were taken into consideration.

First. Characteristics of technique of goalscoring shots in 18-yard box (see the table).

Characteristic of goalscoring shots performed in open play in 18-yard box

Amount of goals (as %), scored by	
leg – 75-80	head – 20-25
Amount of goals (as % of number of goals, scored by leg), scored by leg	
first touch – 65-75	after touch – 25-35
Amount of goals (as % of number of goals, scored by leg), scored after a kick of ball that placed	
on the surface of the pitch – 60-65	at different heights above the surface of the field – 35-40
Amount of goals (as % of number of goals, scored by leg), scored by leg from the position	
in front of goal – 33-37	at an angle with the goal – 63-67
Amount of goals (as %), scored with shots	
with fall – 15-20	without fall – 80-85
Amount of goals (as %), scored with shots	
at the rebound – 10	not at the rebound – 90

Second. Areas of performing of goalscoring shots in 18-yard box.

Majority of goals scored by leg in open play in 18-yard box are scored from an area of oval shape that lies at a distance of 2 meters from the goal line to the 18-yard box line, approximately 25 meters wide and marginally deposed to the right relating to goal (fig. 3).

From 80 to 90% of goals scored by head are scored from an area with dimensions of 10x10 meters that lies opposite to goal at a distance of 2 to 12 meters from the goal line (fig. 4).

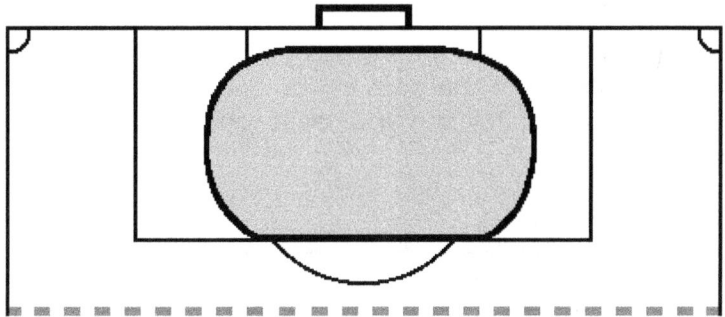

Fig. 3. The area in 18-yard box from which the majority of goals by leg in open play are scored

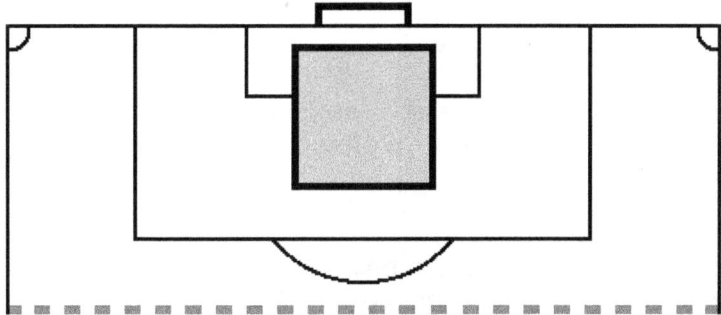

Fig. 4. The area in 18-yard box from which the majority of goals by head are scored

Third. Areas and specificity of performance in competitive games of those actions in 18-yard box or near it which precede directly the goalscoring shots (of assists and movements with the ball resulting in goal).

Assists in 18-yard box performed from two areas, each located to the right and to the left of goal properly between the touchline of 18-yard box and the touchline of the goal area closest to it and extended to the 18-yard box line.

Overwhelmingly balls are sent on short and middle distances in parallel to the goal line and in the diagonal direction to the goal or away from the goal both with crossing the central longitudinal axis of the pitch and without it.

The area in which generally balls are usually sent is located opposite to the goal between the line of the goal area and 18-yard box line and has a width of 13-15 meters (fig. 5).

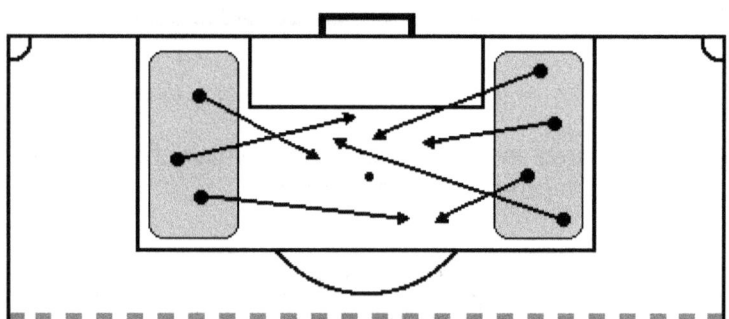

Fig. 5. Areas from which assists in 18-yard box are performed usually and preferential directions of such assists

Movements with the ball in 18-yard box finishing with goalscoring shot performed on small distances in following directions:

– perpendicularly and at a little angle with the goal line between side lines of 18-yard box and side lines of goal area extended onto the pitch, in areas situated between the angles of goal area and 18-yard box (balls are forwarded into the goal at some angle in regard to the direction of movement before the shot);

– in parallel and at some angle with the goal line away from the in areas situated between the angles of goal area and the 18-yard box (balls are forwarded into the goal at a sufficiently large angle in regard to the direction of movement before the shot);

– perpendicularly and at a little angle in regard to the goal line in a «channel» of 15 meters wide approximately, situated in front of goal area between the 18-yard box line and the penalty spot (balls are forwarded into the goal at the direction coinciding with the direction of dribbling, or at some angle in regard to the direction of movement before the shot) (fig. 6).

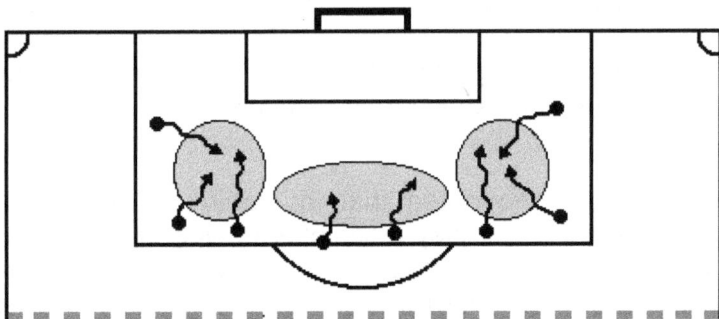

Fig. 6. Preferential directions of movement with the ball in the 18-yard box finished with a goalscoring shot

Given the specifics in technique of performing of attacking actions in 18-yard box in games of highly qualified teams, regularity of scoring in football and the transfer of fitness in precision and speed of actions with the ball there are six allocated sections of gaming drills with the contiguous goals for play technique training in 18-yard box.

Drills of each section naturally have similarities from the point of view of conditions of players actions, but differ in that suppose performance of definite attacking actions with the ball in the 18-yard box to a greater extent (fig. 7).

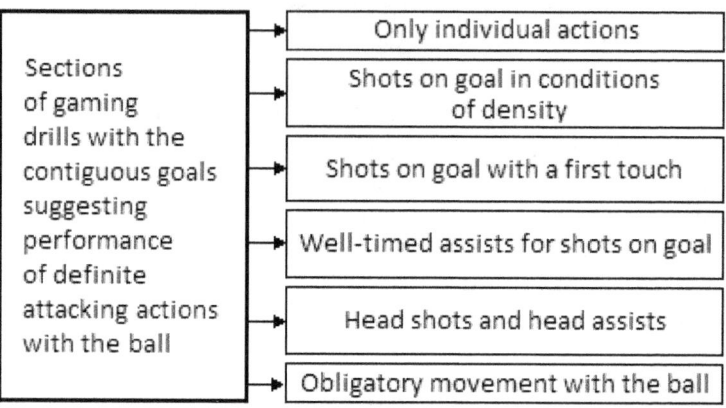

Fig. 7. Sections of gaming drills with the contiguous goals for play technique training in the 18-yard box

It should be noted that in gaming drills with the contiguous goals for play technique training in the 18-yard box players, in contrast to definite attacking actions, are naturally forced to execute some defending actions which in their turn differ from defending actions outside the 18-yard box.

2.2. Drills examples

Section 1. Drills that involve only individual actions

Task № 1	
Task description	Requirements for quality of the task execution
One on one play on condition that goalkeepers put the ball into play on the surface of the pitch. Pitch size: 10 meters wide, 10 meters long. 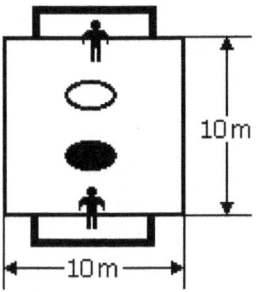 Goalkeepers put the ball into play after catching it or when it is over the goal line and touchlines. Corners are not awarded. Offsides are not given. Players are permitted to pass the ball to goalkeepers only when it put into play after fouls. Goal scored at the rebound counts as two. Play time in one repeat – 1 minute. **Variant:** goals are moved in different directions relative to each other at the goal line	– goalkeepers should put the ball into play without delay; – players should act at maximum intensity; – players should operate with the ball quickly and perform the shooting motion during shots on goal especially fast; – players should shoot on goal from any, even most inconvenient, positions; – players should press for every opportunity to finish off the ball into the net; – during the shots on goal performance players should press for sending the ball into the area of the goal unprotected by the goalkeeper

Task № 2	
Task description	Requirements for quality of the task execution
One on one play on condition that goalkeepers put the ball into play necessarily with the rebound from the surface of the pitch. Pitch size: 10 meters wide, 10 meters long. 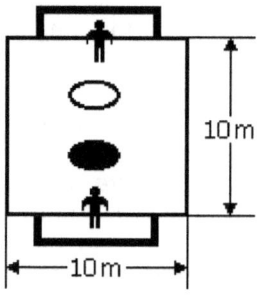 Goalkeepers put the ball into play after catching it or when it is over the goal line and touchlines necessarily with the rebound from the surface of the pitch. Players are permitted to perform shots on goal striking the ball on the surface of the field and bouncing from it. Goal scored by strike on ball in the air counted as two. Players are prohibited to cover the shot by exposing the leg up while the opponent performs shots on goal with ball in the air. Corners are not awarded. Offsides are not given. Players are permitted to pass the ball to goalkeepers only during putting it into play after a foul. Goal scored at the rebound counts as two. Play time in one repeat – 1 minute	– goalkeepers should put the ball into play without delay; – players should act at maximum intensity; – players should operate with the ball quickly and perform the shooting motion during shots on goal especially fast; – players should shoot on goal from any, even most inconvenient, positions; – players should press for every opportunity to finish off the ball into the net; – during the shots on goal performance players should press for sending the ball into the area of the goal unprotected by the goalkeeper; – when opponents perform shots on ball in the air, players should throw their body to prevent the shot

Section 2. Drills that involve shots on goal by leg in conditions of players density

Task № 1	
Task description	Requirements for quality of the task execution
Two on two play. Pitch size: 12 meters wide, 12 meters long. 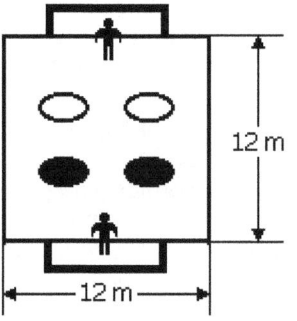 Goalkeepers put the ball into play after catching it or when it is over the goal line and touchlines. Number of passes for players in field during attack – not more than two. Corners are not awarded. Offsides are not given. Goal scored with a first touch counts as two. Goal scored at the rebound counts as two. Play time in one repeat – 2 minutes. **Variant:** goalkeepers put the ball into play with a rebound from the surface of the pitch. Goal scored with strike on ball in the air counts as two	– goalkeepers should put the ball into play without delay; – players should act at maximum intensity; – players should operate with the ball quickly and perform the shooting motion during shots on goal especially fast; – players should interact with partners quickly; – in conditions of space deficit players should look for an opportunity for a shot on goal rather than move with the ball into free space; – players should press for every opportunity to finish off the ball into the net; – during the shots on goal performance players should press for sending the ball into the area of the goal unprotected by the goalkeeper

Task № 2	
Task description	Requirements for quality of the task execution
Two on two play with «neutral» player who plays for attacking team all the time provided that all players act in midfield. Pitch size: 15 meters wide, 30 meters long. On the pitch there are middle zone 10 meters long and goal no further than 5 meters from the goal line. Players act in the middle zone all the time. 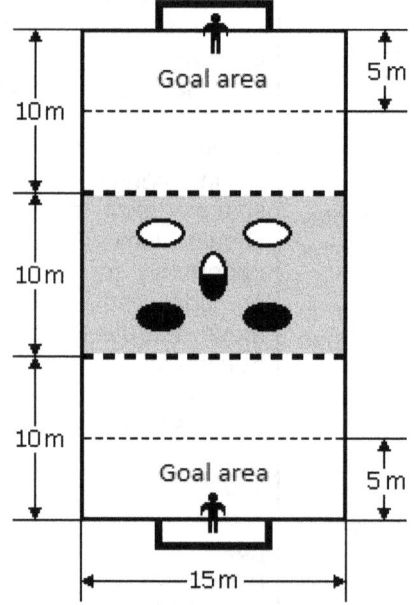 On a signal goalkeepers put the ball into play to the middle zone from the goal area after catching it or when it is over the goal line and touchlines.	– players should receive the ball from the goalkeeper within short period of time after a signal for putting the ball into play; – players should use different techniques of opening for receiving the ball from goalkeeper and partners in the most comfortable position; – players of defending team should intercept the ball during the pass performance by the goalkeeper or attack the opponent at the moment of reception of the ball entering into physical contact with him; – goalkeepers and players should pass the ball to partner timely and accurately, giving him time for performance of shot on goal; – players should interact with partners quickly;

SOCCER. Gaming drills with the contiguous goals for play technique training

Task № 2 continuation

Task description	Requirements for quality of the task execution
Players from attacking team tend to outplay players from defending team and perform shot on goal from the middle zone. Number of passes made by players during the attack – no more than three. Players from attacking team are permitted to finish off the ball into the net outside the middle zone. Goal scored in this manner count as two. Players from defending team tend to prevent players from attacking team from shot on goal. Corners are not awarded. Offsides are not given. Goal scored with a first touch counts as two. Play time in one repeat – 5 minutes. **Variant:** players act as goalkeepers, they are permitted to protect the goal with any body part except hands. **Note.** While changing the length of areas between the goal line and the middle zone there may be established conditions for players to perform shots on goal from the greater or smaller distances and for goalkeepers (players act as goalkeepers) to pass the ball on greater or smaller distances	– players from defending team should attack a player from attacking team who has possessed the ball as quickly as possible, forcing him to act in conditions of time and space deficit; – players should operate with the ball quickly and perform a strike while shooting on goal exceptionally quick; – players should shoot on goal from any position, even the most inconvenient; – players should try to use any opportunity to finish off the ball into the net; – performing shots on goal players should try to send the ball into goal area unprotected by the goalkeeper

Task № 3	
Task description	Requirements for quality of the task execution
Two on two play with the «neutral» player who plays for attacking team all the time. Pitch size: 15 meters wide, 12 meters long. 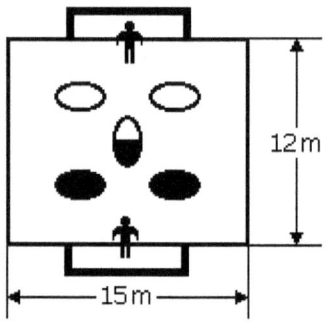 Goalkeepers put the ball into play on the surface after catching it or when it is over the goal line and touchlines. Number of passes for players during the attack – no more than two. Corners are not awarded. Offsides are not given. Goal scored with a first touch counts as two. Goal scored at the rebound counts as two. Play time in one repeat – 5 minutes. **Variant:** goalkeepers put the ball into play with the rebound from the surface. Goal scored with the strike in the ball in the air counts as two	– goalkeepers should put the ball into play without a delay; – players should act at a maximum intensity; – players should operate with the ball quickly and perform a strike while shooting on goal exceptionally quick; – players should interact with partners quickly; – in conditions of space deficit players should search for an opportunity to shoot on goal and shouldn't move with the ball on a free space; – players should try to use every opportunity to finish off the ball into the net; – performing shots on goal players should try to send the ball into goal area unprotected by the goalkeeper

SOCCER. Gaming drills with the contiguous goals for play technique training

Task № 4	
Task description	Requirements for quality of the task execution
Three on three play. Pitch size: 16 meters wide, 16 meters long. 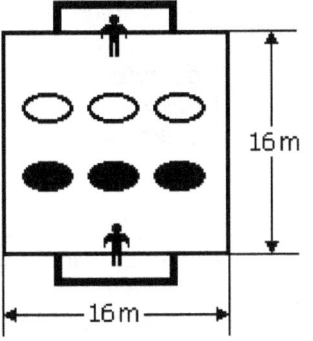 Goalkeepers put the ball into play on the surface after catching it or when it is over the goal line and touchlines. Number of passes for players during the attack – no more than two. Corners are not awarded. Offsides are not given. Goal scored with a first touch counts as two. Goal scored at the rebound counts as two. Play time in one repeat – 3 minutes. **Variants:** a) middle line of the pitch is marked, offsides are given; b) goalkeepers put the ball into play with the rebound from the surface; c) goals are moved in different directions relative to each other at the goal line	– goalkeepers should put the ball into play without a delay; – players should act at a maximum intensity; – players should operate with the ball quickly and perform a strike while shooting on goal exceptionally quick; – players should interact with partners quickly; – in conditions of space deficit players should search for an opportunity to shoot on goal and shouldn't move with the ball on a free space; – players should shoot on goal from any position, even the most inconvenient; – players should try to use every opportunity to finish off the ball into the net; – performing shots on goal players should try to send the ball into goal area unprotected by the goalkeeper

27

Task № 5	
Task description	Requirements for quality of the task execution
Three on three play with the «neutral» player who plays for the attacking team all the time. Pitch size: 20 meters wide, 16 meters long. 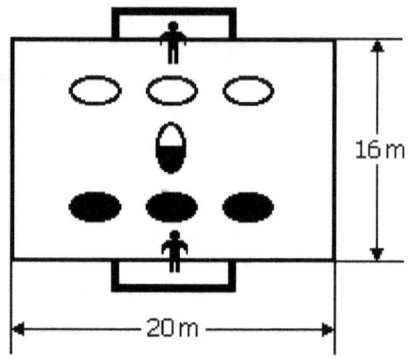 Goalkeepers put the ball into play on the surface after catching it or when it is over the goal line and touchlines. Number of passes for players during the attack – no more than two. Corners are not awarded. Offsides are not given. Goal scored with a first touch counts as two. Goal scored at the rebound counts as two. Play time in one repeat – 5 minutes. **Variants:** a) goalkeepers put the ball into play with the rebound from the surface; b) goals are moved in different directions relative to each other at the goal line	– goalkeepers should put the ball into play without a delay; – players should act at a maximum intensity; – players should operate with the ball quickly and perform a strike while shooting on goal exceptionally quick; – players should interact with partners quickly; – in conditions of space deficit players should search for an opportunity to shoot on goal and shouldn't move with the ball on a free space; – players should shoot on goal from any position, even the most inconvenient; – players should try to use every opportunity to finish off the ball into the net; – performing shots on goal players should try to send the ball into goal area unprotected by the goalkeeper

SOCCER. Gaming drills with the contiguous goals for play technique training

Section 3. Drills intending shots on goal by leg with the first touch

Task № 1	
Task description	Requirements for quality of the task execution
Three on three play providing shots on goal with a first touch. Pitch size: 20 meters wide, 16 meters long. [diagram: pitch 20m × 16m with two goals and six players] Goalkeepers put the ball into play after catching it or when it is over the goal line and touchlines. Shots on goal are performed necessarily with a first touch. Number of passes for players during the attack – no more than three. Corners are not awarded. Offsides are not given. Goal scored at the rebound counts as two. Play time in one repeat – 3 minutes	– goalkeepers should put the ball into play without a delay; – players should begin preparation of shot on goal timely relative to the moment when partner who possesses the ball is ready to perform a pass; – players should perform passes for shots on goal as precisely as possible («at the feet»); – players should shoot on goal from any position, even the most inconvenient; – players should try to use every opportunity to finish off the ball into the net; – performing shots on goal players should try to send the ball into goal area unprotected by the goalkeeper

Task № 2	
Task description	Requirements for quality of the task execution
Three on three play with the «neutral» player who plays for attacking team all the time providing shots on goal with a first touch. Pitch size: 30 meters wide, 20 meters long. There are three zones marked in the pitch: two lateral 6 meters wide and the middle 18 meters wide. 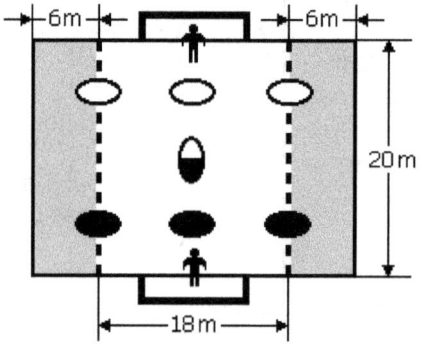 Goalkeepers put the ball into play after catching it or when it is over the goal line and touchlines. Shots on goal are performed necessarily from the middle zone with a **first touch** after a pass from the lateral zone. Number of passes for players during the attack – no more than three. Corners are not awarded. Offsides are not given. Goal scored at the rebound counts as two. Play time in one repeat – 5 minutes	– goalkeepers should put the ball into play without a delay; – players should begin preparation of shot on goal timely relative to the moment when partner who possesses the ball is ready to perform a pass; – players should perform passes for shots on goal as precisely as possible («at the feet»); – players should shoot on goal from any position, even the most inconvenient; – players should try to use every opportunity to finish off the ball into the net; – performing shots on goal players should try to send the ball into goal area unprotected by the goalkeeper

SOCCER. Gaming drills with the contiguous goals for play technique training

Task № 3	
Task description	Requirements for quality of the task execution
Four on four play providing shots on goal with a first or a second touch. Pitch size: 16 meters wide, 16 meters long. 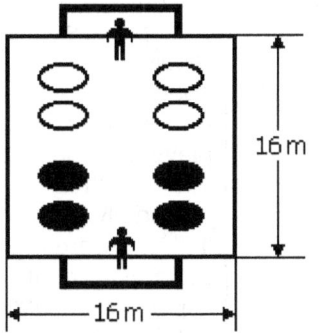 Goalkeepers put the ball into play after catching it or when it is over the goal line and touchlines necessarily with a mounted trajectory. Players from attacking team try to make a pass with a head or a leg to a partner for shot on goal with a **first touch** by head or leg. Goal scored in that manner counts as three. Players are permitted to shoot on goal with a second touch. Corners are not awarded. Offsides are not given. Players are permitted to pass the ball to goalkeepers. Goal scored at the rebound counts as two. Play time in one repeat – 5 minutes	– goalkeepers should put the ball into play without a delay and necessarily with a mounted trajectory; – players should try to win the ball after goalkeeper put it into play with a mounted trajectory; – players should try to perform passes and shots on goal in conditions of physical contact with an opponent; – players should shoot on goal with head and leg from any position, even the most inconvenient; – players should try to use every opportunity to finish off the ball into the net; – performing shots on goal players should try to send the ball into goal area unprotected by the goalkeeper

Section 4. Drills implying obligatory movements with the ball

Task № 1	
Task description	Requirements for quality of the task execution
Two on two play with a «neutral» player who plays for attacking team all the time providing prohibition of «play in one and two touches». Pitch size: 15 meters wide, 20 meters long. 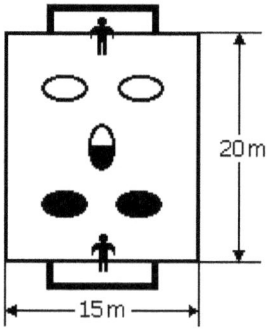 Goalkeepers put the ball into play after catching it or when it is over the goal line and touchlines. Players are prohibited to play in one and two touches except in case of finishing off the ball into the net. They should operate with the ball in particular situation by the same leg they touched the ball in this situation. Number of passes by players during the attack – no more than two. Corners are not awarded. Offsides are not given. Play time in one repeat – 5 minutes	– goalkeepers should put the ball into play without a delay; – players should receive the ball with an «outgoing»; – receiving the ball players should switch into the game powerfully, moving with it towards the opponent's goal; – players should try to outplay the opponent bravely; – players should operate with the ball quickly and perform a strike while shooting on goal exceptionally quick; – players should shoot on goal from any position, even the most inconvenient; – players should try to use every opportunity to finish off the ball into the net; – performing shots on goal players should try to send the ball into goal area unprotected by the goalkeeper

SOCCER. Gaming drills with the contiguous goals for play technique training

Task № 2	
Task description	Requirements for quality of the task execution
Two on two play with a «neutral» player who plays for attacking team all the time providing shots on goal from the defensive zone and prohibition of «play in one and two touches». Pitch size: 20 meters wide, 16 meters long. Half-way line which divides pitch into attacking and defensive zones is marked. 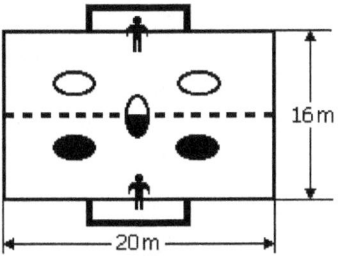 Goalkeepers put the ball into play after catching it or when it is over the goal line and touchlines. Players are prohibited to play in one and two touches except in case of finishing off the ball into the net. They should operate with the ball in particular situation by the same leg they touched the ball in this situation and shoot on goal from the defensive zone exceptionally. Number of passes by players during the attack – no more than two. Players are permitted to finish off the ball into the net in the attacking zone. Corners are not given. Play time in one repeat – 3 minutes	– goalkeepers should put the ball into play without a delay; – players should receive the ball with an «outgoing»; – receiving the ball players should switch into the game powerfully, moving with it towards the opponent's goal; – players should try to outplay the opponent bravely; – players should operate with the ball quickly and perform a strike while shooting on goal exceptionally quick; – players should shoot on goal from any position, even the most inconvenient; – players should try to use every opportunity to finish off the ball into the net; – performing shots on goal players should try to send the ball into goal area unprotected by the goalkeeper

Section 5. Drills implying timely passes for shots on goal

Task № 1	
Task description	Requirements for quality of the task execution
Three on three play providing two players of a team act in defensive zone and one in attacking zone all the time. Pitch size: 15 meters wide, 18 meters long. There are three zones marked on the pitch: of attack and defense each 7 meters long, and middle 4 meters long. Two players from each team act in defensive zone of their team, and one in attacking zone all the time. Players are prohibited from moving from zone to zone. 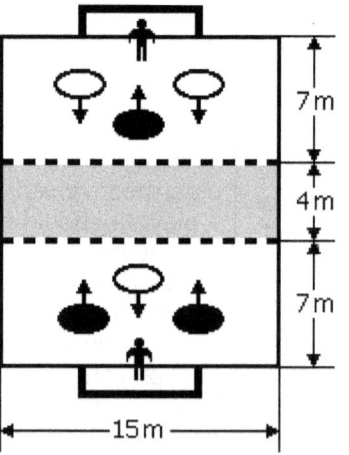 Goalkeepers put the ball into play after catching it or when it is over the goal line and touchlines.	– goalkeepers should put the ball into play without a delay; – player from defending team acting in opponents' defensive zone should attack opponent who received the ball as quickly as possible, forcing him to act in conditions of time and space deficit; – players should pass the ball to partner timely and precisely, providing him with the time for a shot on goal; – player from attacking team acting in attacking zone should shade the visibility for goalkeeper and change the direction of the ball when his partners shoot on goal; – players should operate with the ball quickly and perform a strike while shooting on goal exceptionally quickly;

Task № 1 continuation

Task description	Requirements for quality of the task execution
Two players from the attacking team acting in defensive zone try to outplay a player from the defending team and shoot on goal from this zone. Number of passes by players during the attack – no more than two. Player from the attacking team acting in attacking zone tries to shade the visibility for goalkeeper, change the direction of the ball, finish off the ball into the net. Player from the defending team acting in defensive zone of the opponents' team tries to take the ball off and pass it to his partners into defensive zone of his team. Corners are not awarded. Offsides are not given. Goal scored with a first touch counts as two. Goal scored at the rebound counts as two. Play time in one repeat – 5 minutes. **Variants:** a) player of the defending team acting in defensive zone of opponents' team is permitted to shoot on goal in case of taking off the ball; b) players of the attacking team acting in defensive zone are permitted to shoot on goal from the middle zone in falling	– players should shoot on goal from any position, even the most inconvenient; – players should shoot on goal including shots with a first touch; – player from the attacking team acting in attacking zone should try to use every opportunity to finish off the ball into the net; – performing shots on goal players should try to send the ball into goal area unprotected by the goalkeeper

Task № 2	
Task description	Requirements for quality of the task execution
Two on two play with two «neutral» players who play for the attacking team all the time providing that: **– one players acts in defensive zone, and another – in attacking zone;** **– one «neutral» player acts in defensive zone, and another – in attacking zone.** Pitch size: 15 meters wide, 18 meters long. There are three zones marked on the pitch: of attack and defense 7 meters long each, and middle 4 meters long. There is one player in each team who acts in his team defensive zone all the time, and another – in attacking zone. One «neutral» player acts in defensive zone, and the other – in attacking zone all the time. Switch between the zones is prohibited. 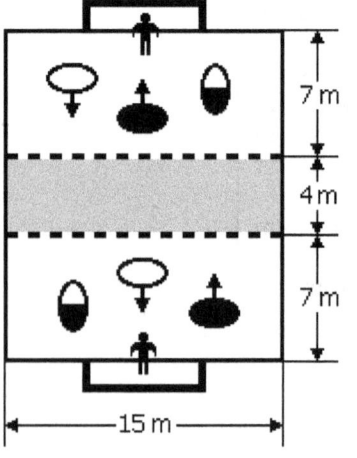	– goalkeepers should put the ball into play without a delay; – player from defending team acting in opponents' defensive zone should attack opponent who received the ball as quickly as possible, forcing him to act in conditions of time and space deficit; – players should pass the ball to partner timely and precisely, providing him with the time for a shot on goal; – player from attacking team acting in attacking zone should shade the visibility for goalkeeper and change the direction of the ball when his partners shoot on goal; – players should operate with the ball quickly and perform a strike while shooting on goal exceptionally quickly; – players should shoot on goal from any position, even the most inconvenient;

SOCCER. Gaming drills with the contiguous goals for play technique training

Task № 2 continuation

Task description	Requirements for quality of the task execution
Goalkeepers put the ball into play after catching it or when it is over the goal line and touchlines. Player from the attacking team and «neutral» player acting in defensive zone of attacking team try to outplay one player from the defending team and shoot on goal from this zone. Number of passes by these players to each other – no more than three. Player from the attacking team and «neutral» player acting in attacking zone try to shade the visibility for goalkeeper, change the direction of the ball, shoot on goal in case of picking-up the ball after partners shots from defensive zone and during finishing off the ball into the net. Number of passes by these players to each other during the attack – no more than one. Player of the defending team acting in defensive zone of opponents' team tries to take off the ball and shoot on goal. Corners are not awarded. Offsides are not given. Goal scored at the rebound counts as two. Play time in one repeat – 5 minutes	– players should shoot on goal including shots with a first touch; – player from the attacking team acting in attacking zone should try to use every opportunity to finish off the ball into the net; – performing shots on goal players should try to send the ball into goal area unprotected by the goalkeeper

Task № 3	
Task description	Requirements for quality of the task execution
Three on three play with goals mounted diagonally to each other providing that two players act in defensive zone and one in attacking zone all the time. Pitch size: 16 meters wide, 14 meters long. There are three zones marked on the pitch: of attack and defense 6 meters long each, and the middle 2 meters long. Goals are moved in different directions relative to each other at the goal line and mounted by the corners of the pitch. In each team there are two players act in defensive zone of their team, and one – in attacking zone all the time. Players are prohibited from moving from zone to zone. 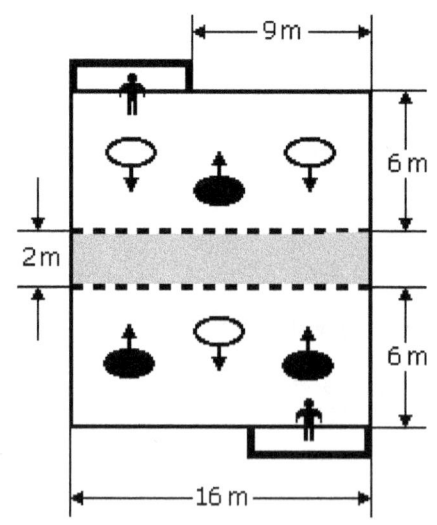	– goalkeepers should put the ball into play without a delay; – player from defending team acting in opponents' defensive zone should attack opponent who received the ball as quickly as possible, forcing him to act in conditions of time and space deficit; – players should pass the ball to partner timely and precisely, providing him with the time for a shot on goal; – player from attacking team acting in attacking zone should shade the visibility for goalkeeper and change the direction of the ball when his partners shoot on goal; – players should operate with the ball quickly and perform a strike while shooting on goal exceptionally quickly; – players should shoot on goal from any position, even the most inconvenient;

Task № 3 continuation

Task description	Requirements for quality of the task execution
Goalkeepers put the ball into play after catching it or when it is over the goal line and touchlines. Players from the attacking team acting in defensive zone try to outplay player from the defending team and shoot on goal from this zone. Number of passes by these players to each other – no more than two. Player from the attacking team acting in attacking zone tries to shade the visibility for goalkeeper, change the direction of the ball, finish off the ball into the net. Player of the defending team acting in defensive zone of opponents' team tries to take off the ball and shoot on goal. Corners are not awarded. Offsides are not given. Goal scored with a first touch counts as two. Goal scored at the rebound counts as two. Play time in one repeat – 5 minutes. **Variants:** a) players of the attacking team acting in defensive zone are permitted to shoot on goal from the middle zone in falling; b) goalkeepers put the ball into play with a rebound from the pitch surface	– players should shoot on goal including shots with a first touch; – player from the attacking team acting in attacking zone should try to use every opportunity to finish off the ball into the net; – performing shots on goal players should try to send the ball into goal area unprotected by the goalkeeper

Task № 4	
Task description	Requirements for quality of the task execution
Four attacking players on two defending players play in two zones, situated at some distance from each other, providing passes from zone to zone and during local movements. There are two zones marked on the pitch 10 meters wide and 15 meters long, with longer sides opposite each other at a distance of 5 meters. Goals are mounted on opposite shorter sides of different zones. There are two attacking and one defending player acting in each zone all the time. Players are permitted from moving from zone to zone. 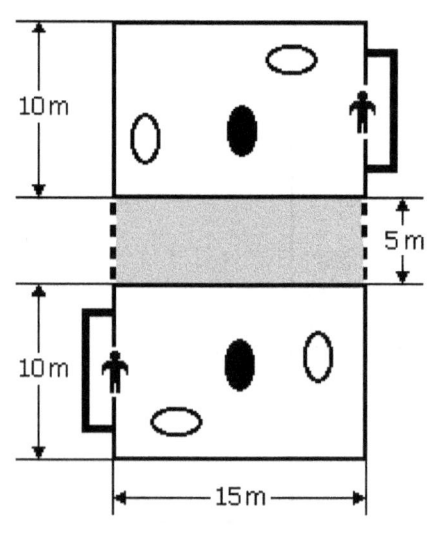	– goalkeepers should put the ball into play without a delay; – defending players should try to intercept balls or attack opponent during the ball reception entering into a physical contact with him; – attacking players acting in one zone should pass the ball to each other timely and precisely, providing partner with time to pass into opposite zone; – defending players should attack opponent who received the ball as quickly as possible, forcing him to act in conditions of time and space deficit; – attacking players receiving the ball from other zone should try to finish the attack with shot on goal quickly; – attacking players located in different zones should act simultaneously in attempts to deliver the ball from zone to zone;

SOCCER. Gaming drills with the contiguous goals for play technique training

Task № 4 continuation

Task description	Requirements for quality of the task execution
Goalkeepers put the ball into play in zone where goals they protect are situated, after catching it or when it is over the goal line and touchlines. Two attacking players try to pass the ball to partners in opposite zone for shot on goal. Number of passes by attacking players to each other after receiving ball from the goalkeeper before sending it into the opposite zone – no more than two. Number of passes by attacking players to each other after receiving ball from the goalkeeper before shots on goal – no more than two. One of defending players tries to prevent attacking players from passing the ball into the opposite zone, and another – from shooting on goal. The aim for four attacking players is to score as much goals as possible within a certain time. **Offsides are given.** Goal scored with the first touch counts as two. Goal scored on the rebound counts as two. **Variants:** a) goals are mounted opposite to each other on opposite longer sides of different zones; b) passes from zone to zone are performed necessarily with a mounted trajectory	– players should operate with the ball quickly and perform a strike while shooting on goal exceptionally quickly; – players should shoot on goal from any position, even the most inconvenient; – players should try to use every opportunity to finish off the ball into the net; – performing shots on goal players should try to send the ball into goal area unprotected by the goalkeeper

Task № 5	
Task description	Requirements for quality of the task execution
Four attacking players on two defending players play in two zones, situated at some distance from each other providing passes from zones to zone during fast movements. There are two zones marked on the pitch 10 meters wide and 18 meters long with longer sides opposite to each other at a distance of 5 meters. In each zone goal areas are marked – no further than 5 meters from the goal line. Goals are mounted on opposite shorter sides of different zones. There are two attacking player and one defending player acting all the time in each zone. Players are prohibited from moving from zone to zone. 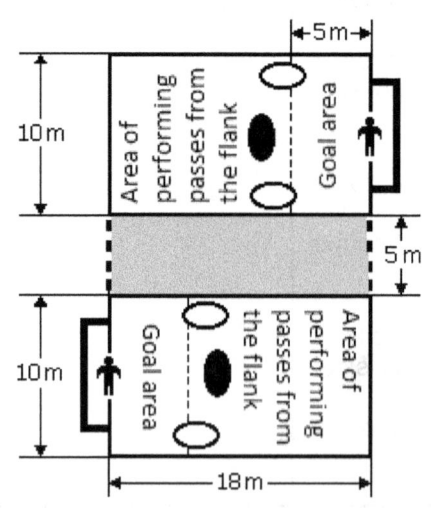	– goalkeepers should put the ball into play without a delay; – defending players should try to intercept balls or attack opponent during the ball reception entering into a physical contact with him; – having received the ball from the goalkeeper, attacking players should try to deliver it to the area of performing passes from the flank quickly and pass it to the opposite zone; – attacking players acting in one zone should pass the ball to each other timely and precisely, providing partner with time to pass the ball into the opposite area; – having received the ball from the other zone, attacking players should try to finish the attack quickly with the shot on goal;

SOCCER. Gaming drills with the contiguous goals for play technique training

Task № 5 continuation

Task description	Requirements for quality of the task execution
Goalkeepers put the ball into play in goal area in the zone where the goal they protect is mounted, after catching it or when it is over the goal line and touchlines. Two attacking players try to deliver the ball from the goal area to the area of performing passes from the flank and pass the ball to partners in opposite zone for shot on goal. Number of passes by attacking players who received the ball from the goalkeeper to each other before sending it to the opposite zone – no more than two. Number of passes by attacking players who received the ball from the opposite zone to each other before the shot on goal – no more than two. One of defending players tries to prevent attacking players from passing the ball into the opposite zone, and another – from shooting on goal. While goalkeeper puts the ball into play defending player acting in this zone stands in goal area. The aim for four attacking players is to score as much goals as possible within a certain time. **Offsides are given.** Goal scored with the first touch counts as two. Goal scored on the rebound counts as two	– attacking players located in different zones should act simultaneously in attempts to deliver the ball from zone to zone; – defending players should attack opponent who received the ball as quickly as possible, forcing him to act in conditions of time and space deficit; – players should operate with the ball quickly and perform a strike while shooting in goal exceptionally quick; – players should shoot on goal from any position, even the most inconvenient; – players should try to use every opportunity to finish off the ball into the net; – performing shots on goal players should try to send the ball into goal area unprotected by the goalkeeper

Task № 6	
Task description	Requirements for quality of the task execution
Three on three play with the «neutral» player playing for attacking team all the time providing all players are situated in middle zone of the pitch at the initial position. Pitch size: 20 meters wide, 25 meters long. There are zones marked on the pitch: of attack and defense 10 meters long each, and the middle 5 meters long. In attacking and defensive zones there are goal areas marked – no further than 5 meters from the goal line. At the initial position players stand in the middle zone. 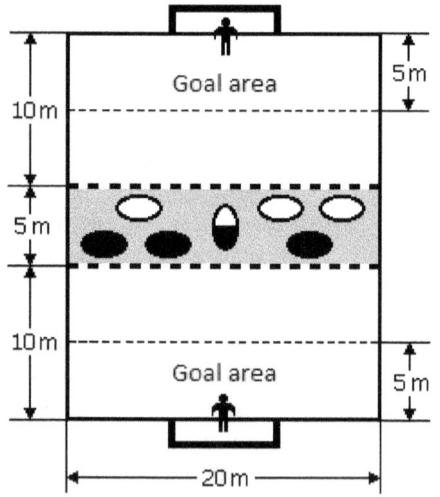 On a signal goalkeepers put the ball into play to the middle zone from the goal area after catching it or when it is over the goal line and touchlines.	– players should receive the ball from the goalkeeper within short period of time after a signal for putting the ball into play; – players should use different techniques of opening for receiving the ball from goalkeeper and partners in the most comfortable position; – players of defending team should intercept the ball during the pass performance by the goalkeeper or attack the opponent at the moment of reception of the ball entering into physical contact with him; – goalkeepers and players should pass the ball to partner timely and accurately, providing him with time for performance of shot on goal; – players should interact with partners quickly;

SOCCER. Gaming drills with the contiguous goals for play technique training

Task № 6 continuation

Task description	Requirements for quality of the task execution
Players from attacking team try to outplay players from defending team and perform shot on goal from the middle zone. Number of passes made by players during the attack – no more than three. Players from defending team try to prevent players from attacking team from shot on goal and knock the ball out of the middle zone and attacking zone. In case of finishing of attack, catching the ball by the goalkeeper and knocking the ball out of middle zone and their zone by players from the defending team all players take their initial positions in the middle zone. Corners are not awarded. **Offsides are given in the attacking zone.** Goal scored with a first touch counts as two. Goal scored at the rebound counts as two. Play time in one repeat – 10 minutes. **Variants:** a) goals are moved in different directions relative to each other at the goal line; b) players act as goalkeepers, they are permitted to protect the goal with any body part except hands; c) four on four play	– defending players should attack opponent who received the ball as quickly as possible, forcing him to act in conditions of time and space deficit; – players should operate with the ball quickly and perform a strike while shooting in goal exceptionally quick; – players should shoot on goal from any position, even the most inconvenient; – players should try to use every opportunity to finish off the ball into the net; – performing shots on goal players should try to send the ball into goal area unprotected by the goalkeeper

Section 6. Drills implying shots on goal and passes by the head

Task № 1	
Task description	Requirements for quality of the task execution
Six attacking players on two defending players play in two zones situated at some distance from each other providing passes from zone to zone with a mounted trajectory. There are two zones marked on the pitch 10 meters wide and 15 meters long at a distance of 10 meters from each other. Goals are mounted on opposite shorter sides of different zones. There are three attacking and one defending zone acting in each zone all the time. Players are permitted from moving from zone to zone. 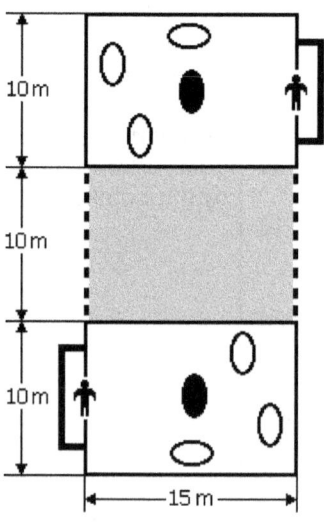	– goalkeepers should put the ball into play without a delay; – players of defending team should intercept the ball during the pass performance by the goalkeeper or attack the opponent at the moment of reception of the ball entering into physical contact with him; – attacking players acting in the same zone should pass the ball to each other timely and precisely, providing partner with time for performance of pass into the opposite zone; – defending players should attack opponent who received the ball as quickly as possible, forcing him to act in conditions of time and space deficit; – players should send the ball purposefully into the opposite zone with a mounted trajectory;

SOCCER. Gaming drills with the contiguous goals for play technique training

Task № 1 continuation

Task description	Requirements for quality of the task execution
Goalkeepers put the ball into the zone where the goal they defend are situated after catching it or when it leaves this zone. Three attacking players try to pass the ball into the opposite zone necessarily with a **mounted trajectory** so that partner can perform shot on goal with a head or a pass with a head for shot on goal with a head or a leg. Number of passes by attacking players having received the ball from the goalkeeper to each other before sending it into the opposite zone – no more than two. Number of passes by attacking players having received the ball from the opposite zone to each other before shot on goal – no more than one. One of defending players tries to prevent attacking players from passing the ball into the opposite zone, and another – to shoot on goal. The aim for six attacking players is to score as much goals as possible within a certain time. Offsides are not given. Goal scored with a first touch counts as two. Goal scored at the rebound counts as two. **Variant:** four attacking players on two defending players	– attacking players located in different zones should act simultaneously in attempts to deliver the ball from zone to zone; – players should shoot on goal and passes with a head from any position, even the most inconvenient; – players should perform shots on goal and passes with a head including the physical contact with the opponent; – players should try to use every opportunity to finish off the ball into the net; – performing shots on goal players should try to send the ball into goal area unprotected by the goalkeeper

Task № 2	
Task description	Requirements for quality of the task execution
Three on three play with three «neutral» players playing for attacking team all the time, two of whom act beyond touchlines. Pitch size: 35 meters wide, 25 meters long. Two «neutral» players act beyond touchlines all the time: one on the right and another on the left. 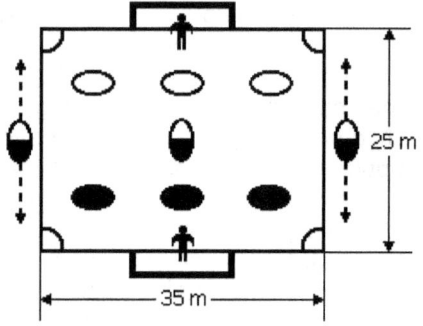 Goalkeepers put the ball into play to players in-field after catching it or when it is over the goal line from players of the attacking team. Players from the attacking team should pass the ball to the one of «neutral» players acting beyond touchlines. Number of passes by attacking players acting in-field to each other before sending it to the «neutral» player acting beyond touchlines – no more than one.	– goalkeepers should put the ball into play without a delay; – having received the players acting in-field should pass it to «neutral» players acting beyond touchlines quickly; – «neutral» players acting beyond touchlines should send the ball to the opponents goal with a mounted trajectory purposefully; – players should shoot on goal and passes with a head from any position, even the most inconvenient; – players should perform shots on goal and passes with a head including the physical contact with the opponent; – players should try to use every opportunity to finish off the ball into the net; – performing shots on goal players should try to send the ball into goal area unprotected by the goalkeeper

Task № 2 continuation

Task description	Requirements for quality of the task execution
«Neutral» players acting beyond touchlines should send the ball to the opponent's goal necessarily with the mounted trajectory so that partners can perform shot on goal with a head or pass for shot on goal with a head or a leg. When the ball is over the goal line of the defending team from the goalkeeper and players of this team, «neutral» players acting beyond touchlines should perform corners necessarily sending the ball to the opponent's goal with a **mounted trajectory.** When the ball is over the touchline, «neutral» players acting beyond touchlines should send the ball by leg to the opponent's goal necessarily with a **mounted trajectory.** Players from the defending team try to prevent players from the attacking team to shoot on goal. Players are permitted to score on the rebound. Goal scored on the rebound counts as two. Offsides are not given. Play time in one repeat – 10 minutes. **Variant:** three on three play with two «neutral» players playing for the attacking team and acting beyond touchlines all the time	

Task № 3	
Task description	Requirements for quality of the task execution
Three on three play with the «neutral» player playing for the attacking team all the time, with goals mounted diagonally to each other. Pitch size: 30 meters wide, 15 meters long. Goals are moved in opposite direction relative to each other on goal line and mounted 5 meters from pitch corners. 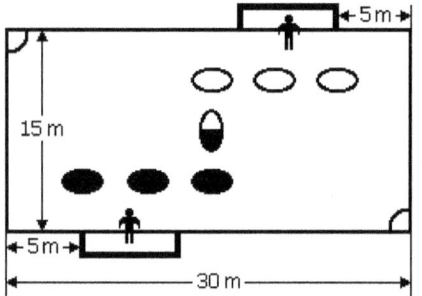 Goalkeepers put the ball into play after catching it or when it is over the goal line from players of attacking team. When the ball is over the touchline players put it into play with hands. Corners are performed from farthest to goal corners of the pitch. Offsides are not given. Goal scored with a head counts as three, and a good ball with a head as one. Goal scored after finishing the ball into the net counts as two. Play time in one repeat – 5 minutes	– goalkeepers should put the ball into play without a delay; – players should search for an opportunity to perform a pass with a mounted trajectory for shot on goal with a head; – players should shoot on goal and passes with a leg and a head from any position, even the most inconvenient; – players should perform shots on goal and passes with a leg and a head including the physical contact with the opponent; – players should try to use every opportunity to finish off the ball into the net; – performing shots on goal players should try to send the ball into goal area unprotected by the goalkeeper

For notes

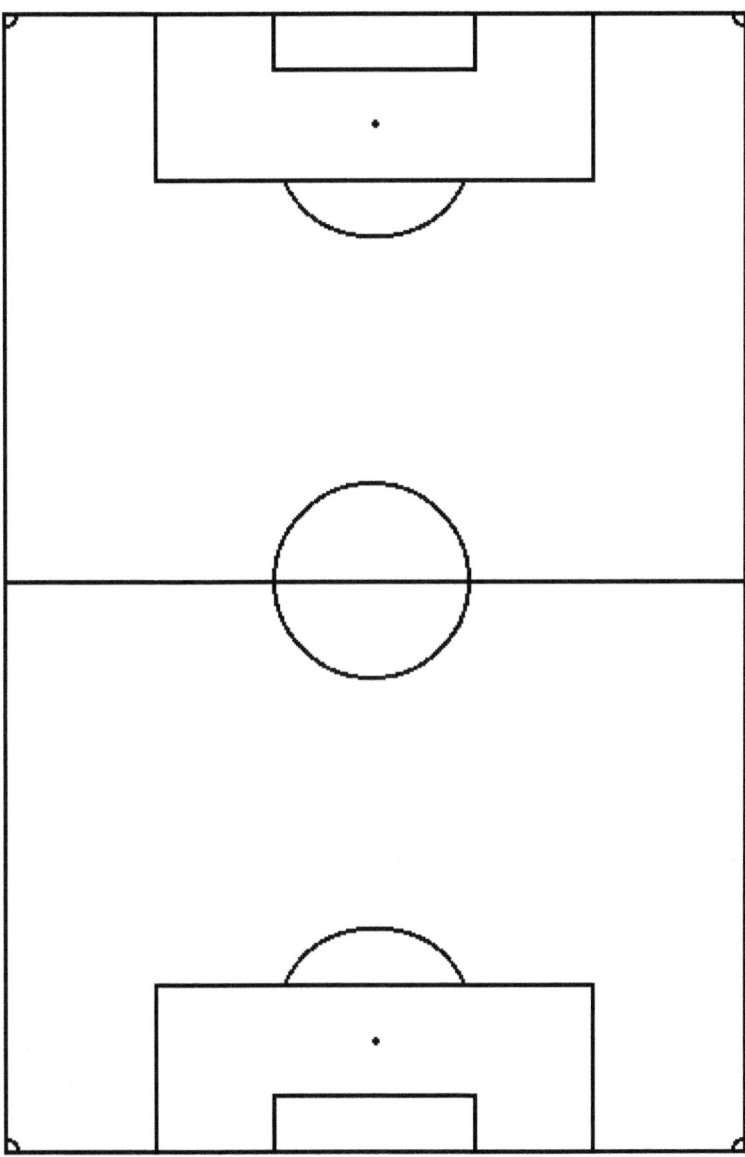

CHAPTER III.
GAMING DRILLS WITH THE CONTIGUOUS GOALS FOR PLAY TECHNIQUE TRAINING IN THE ATTACKING ZONE

3. 1. Drills elaboration

During the elaboration of gaming drills with the contiguous goals for play technique training particularities of the beginning, passing and finishing of goalscoring attacks in competitive games in the current pitch zone.

First. Typical situations in which goals are scored from the outside of the 18-yard box in the context of area of shots performing and players' preparative actions before shots.

From the outside of the 18-yard box goals are scored in open play generally from the area 30 meters wide approximately, situated opposite to the goal within 25 meters from the goal-line of defending team, in such situations principally:

– with a first touch after passes on the pitch surface on the short and medium distance parallel to the 18-yard box line and at different angles to the 18-yard box line in the direction from the goal of defending team;

– with a second touch after reception of the ball sent on the short and medium distance on the pitch surface and high-angle trajectory parallel and at different angles to the 18-yard box line;

– with a third touch after receiving and handling the ball sent on the short and medium distance on the pitch surface and high-angle trajectory parallel and at different angles to the 18-yard box line;

– after moving with the ball on the short and medium distance in the direction of the goal of defending team perpendicular and at different angles to the 18-yard box line both with and without the outplaying of the opponent;

— after moving with the ball on the short and medium distance in the direction of the lateral axis of the pitch something parallel to the 18-yard box line both with and without the outplaying of the opponent.

Second. Areas in the attacking zone in which the last move before the goalscoring shot is performed, and prevailing direction of assists and movements with the ball finishing with the goalscoring shot.

From areas situated between sidelines of the pitch and 18-yard box:
— assists are performed principally with the sending of the ball parallel to the goal-line or closely to this direction into the area situated opposite to the goal at a distance from 4-5 to 12-13 meters from the goal-line (fig. 8);

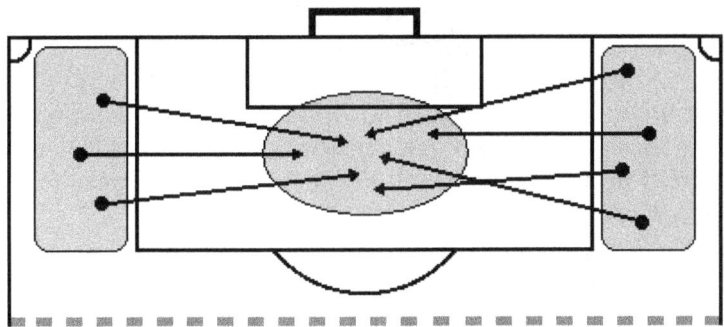

Fig. 8. Prevailing direction of assists into the 18-yard box from areas situated between sidelines of the pitch and 18-yard box

— movements with the ball to the 18-yard box with or without the outplaying of the opponent and with the following goalscoring shot are performed generally on the short and medium distance parallel or at some angle to the goal-line away from the goal in areas situated between angles of the goal area and the 18-yard box (fig. 9).

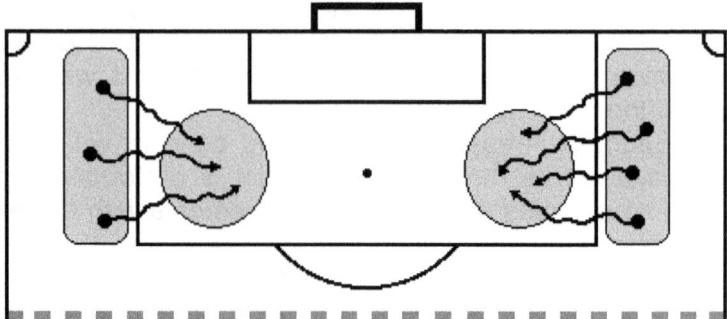

Fig. 9. Prevailing direction of movements with the ball into the 18-yard box finishing with the goalscoring shot from areas situated between touchlines of the pitch and 18-yard box

From the area situated 16-35 meters away from the goal-line of the defending team:
– movements with the ball to the 18-yard box with or without the outplaying of the opponent with the following goalscoring shot are performed generally from areas situated no further than 27-30 meters from the goal-line of the defending team in two directions:

a) perpendicularly or at some angle to the goal-line on the short and medium distance through «corridors» that may be formed as a result of extension of the goal area and 18-yard box sidelines, into areas situated between angles of the goal area and 18-yard box;

b) perpendicularly or at some angle to the goal-line on the short distance in the «corridor» 15 meters wide approximately, situated opposite to the goal area, into the area situated between the 18-yard box line and penalty spot (fig. 10);

– assists into the 18-yard box are performed generally with sending the ball at different angles (with or without the crossing the central longitudinal axis of the pitch) or perpendicularly (or closely to this direction) to the goal-line into the area situated opposite to the goal area between the lines of the 18-yard box and goal area (fig. 11).

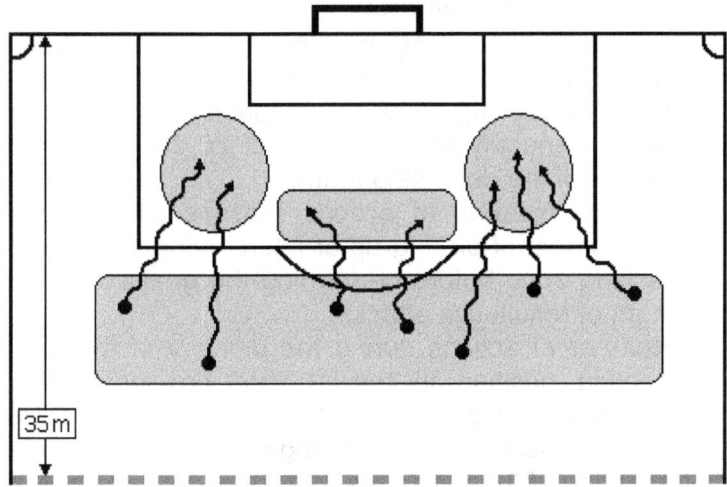

Fig. 10. Prevailing direction of movements with the ball into the 18-yard box finishing with the goalscoring shot from the area situated 16-35 meters away from the goal-line of the defending team

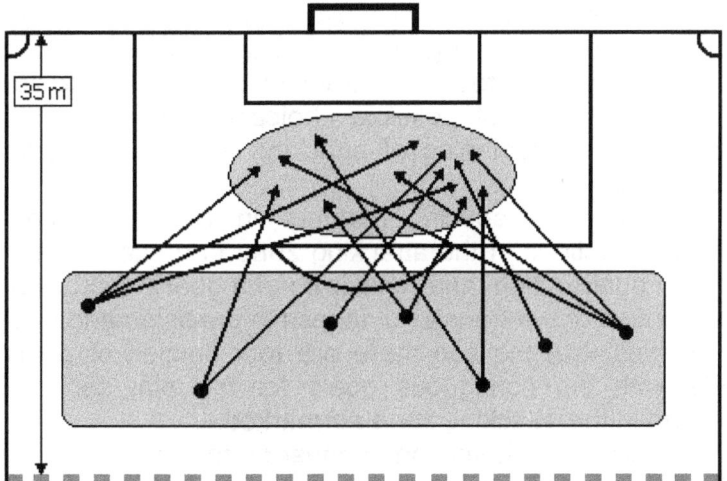

Fig. 11. Prevailing directions of assists into the 18-yard box from the area situated 16-35 meters away from the goal-line of the defending team

Third. Areas of resultative attacks beginning in the attacking zone after picking-up or interception of the ball.

Resultative attacks after taking possession of the ball as a result of picking-up or interception in the attacking zone begin generally at a distance of 20-35 meters from the goal-line of the defending team.

Fourth. Number of actions (passes and dribbling) from the moment of picking-up or interception of the ball in the attacking zone before performing the goalscoring shot and length of resultative attacks.

Number of actions during the delivery of the ball to the shooting position in the 18-yard box or to areas situated beyond the box no further than 25 meters from the goal-line, in resultative attacks beginning after picking-up or interception of the ball in the attacking zone, is generally no more than three. Timing of such attacks is no more than 10 sec.

Fifth. Probability of a goal on case of players possess the ball in the attacking zone is concerned with the speed of decision-making about such action beginning wherein chances to score are the highest.

Therefore the one of main requirements for players during performance of gaming drills with contiguous goals in order to playing technique training in the attacking zone consists in quickest possible choice of the most viable variant of the beginning of attacking actions after taking possession.

Given the specific features in the technique of attacking actions in the attacking zone in games of teams of high qualification, analytical laws of a goal in football and regularities of the transfer of fitness in precision and speed of actions with the ball there are four section of gaming drills with the contiguous goals for the play technique training in the attacking zone earmarked.

Drills of each section suggest performance of certain attacking and subsequently defending actions in the attacking zone, including the 18-yard box (fig. 12).

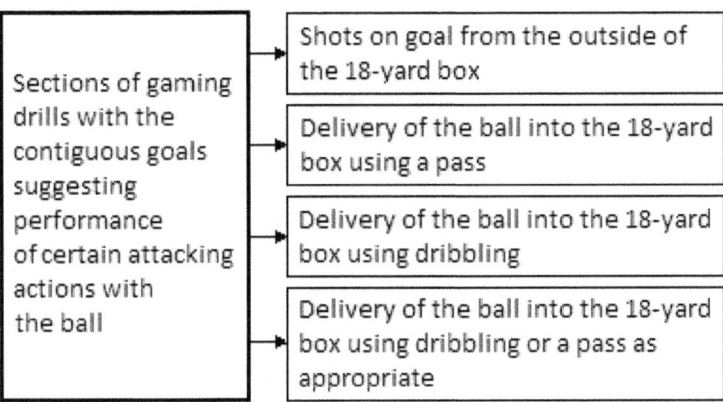

Fig. 12. Sections of gaming drills with the contiguous goals for play technique training in the attacking zone

3. 2. Drills examples

Section 1. Drills suggesting shots on goal from the outside of the 18-yard box

Task № 1	
Task description	Requirements for quality of the task execution
Three on three play providing actions of two team players in the defending zone, and one in the attacking zone all the time. Pitch size: 12 meters wide, 24 meters long. There are three zones marked on the pitch: of attack, defense and the middle, 8 meters long each. In every team two players act in their team defending zone and one – in the attacking zone all the time. Players are not permitted to move from zone to zone. 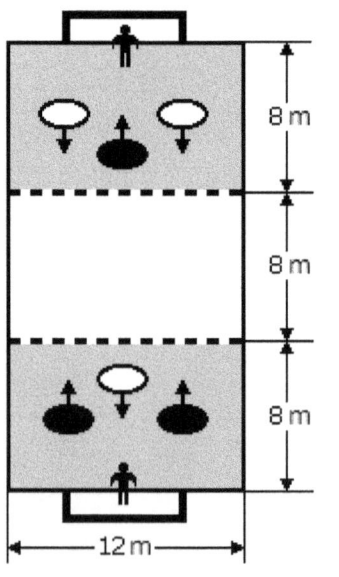	– goalkeepers should put the ball into play without a delay; – player of defending team acting in the attacking zone should attack the opponent who has received the ball as quick as possible, forcing him to act in conditions of time and space deficit; – players should pass the ball to the partner timely and precisely, providing him with time for the shot on goal; – player from attacking team acting in the attacking zone should shade the visibility for goalkeeper and change the direction of the ball when his partners shoot on goal; – players should operate with the ball quickly and perform the shooting motion during shots on goal especially fast;

SOCCER. Gaming drills with the contiguous goals for play technique training

Task № 1 continuation

Task description	Requirements for quality of the task execution
Goalkeepers put the ball into play in their team defending zone after catching it or when it is over the goal-line or sidelines. Two players from the attacking team acting in the defending zone try to outplay one player of the defending team and shoot on goal from this zone. Number of passes by in-field players during the attack is no more than two. Player from attacking team acting in the attacking zone tries to shade the visibility for goalkeeper and change the direction of the ball, finish off the ball into the net. Player from defending team acting in the defending zone of opponents team tries to pick the ball up and shoot on goal or to pass it to partners in his team defending zone. Corners are not awarded. Offsides are not given. Goal scored with a first touch counts as two. Goal scored at the rebound counts as two. Play time in one repeat – 5 minutes. **Variants:** a) goals are moved in different directions relative to each other at the goal line; b) goalkeepers put the ball into play with a rebound from the surface of the pitch	– players should shoot on goal from any, even most inconvenient, positions with a maximum power; – players should soot on goal including shots with a first touch; – player from the attacking team acting in the attacking zone should try to use every opportunity to finish off the ball into the net; – during the shots on goal performance players should press for sending the ball into the area of the goal unprotected by the goalkeeper

Task № 2	
Task description	Requirements for quality of the task execution
Two on two play with a «neutral» player acting for attacking team all the time providing all players acting in the middle zone. Pitch size: 20 meters wide, 40 meters long. Middle zone 8 meters long and areas from which ball is put into the play are marked on the pitch no further than 10 meters from goal-lines. Players act in the middle zone all the time. 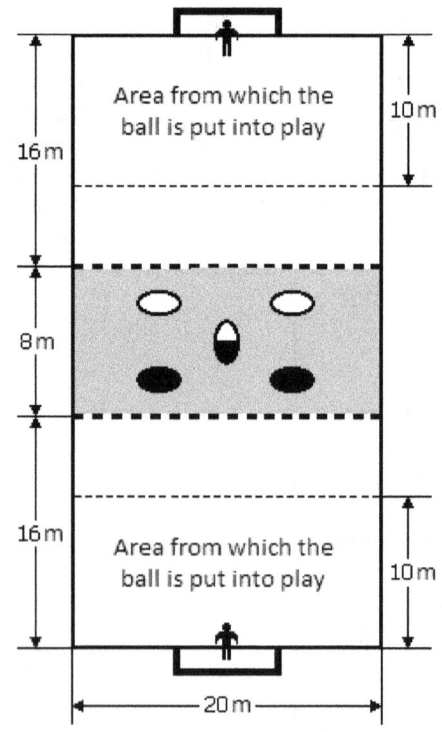	– players should receive the ball from the goalkeeper in the short run after a signal for putting the ball into play; – players should use different opening skills for receiving the ball from the goalkeeper and partners in the most comfortable position; – during pass performance by the goalkeeper players from the defending team should try to intercept the ball or attack the opponent in the moment of reception of the ball coming into a physical contact; – goalkeepers and players should pass the ball to partner timely and accurately, giving him time for performance of shot on goal; – players should interact with partners quickly;

SOCCER. Gaming drills with the contiguous goals for play technique training

Task № 2 continuation

Task description	Requirements for quality of the task execution
On a signal goalkeepers put the ball into play to the middle zone from the «area from which the ball is put into play» after catching it or when it is over the goal-line and touchlines. Players from the attacking team try to outplay players from the defending team and shoot on goal from the middle zone. Number of passes by in-field players during the attack is no more than three. Player from the attacking team are permitted to finish off the ball into the net beyond the middle zone. Goal scored in such manner counts as two. Players from the defending team try to prevent players from attacking team from shot on goal. Corners are not awarded. Offsides are not given. **Variants:** a) players act as goalkeepers, they are permitted to protect the goal with any body part except hands; b) goals are moved in different directions relative to each other at the goal line; в) the length of «areas from which the ball is put into play» for passes by goalkeepers (players acting as goalkeepers) on different distance is varied	– players from the defending team should attack a player from attacking team who has possessed the ball as quickly as possible, forcing him to act in conditions of time and space deficit; – players should operate with the ball quickly and perform the shooting motion during shots on goal especially fast; – players should shoot on goal from any, even most inconvenient, positions with a maximum power; – during the shots on goal performance players should press for sending the ball into the area of the goal unprotected by the goalkeeper

Task № 3	
Task description	Requirements for quality of the task execution
Two on two play with a «neutral» player acting for the attacking team all the time, providing all players actions in attacking and defending zones alternatively. Pitch size: 20 meters wide, 26 meters long. There are three zones marked on the pitch: of attack and defense 10 meters long each and the middle 6 meters long. 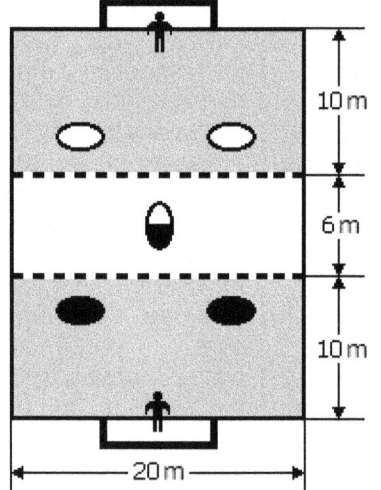 Goalkeepers put the ball into play to the defending zone of their team after catching it or when it is over the goal-line and touchlines. Players from the attacking team try to shoot on goal from the defending zone. Number of passes by in-field players during the attack is no more than three.	– goalkeepers should the ball into play without a delay; – players of defending team should intercept the ball during the pass performance by the goalkeeper or attack the opponent at the moment of reception of the ball entering into physical contact with him; – players should pass the ball to partner timely and accurately, giving him time for performance of shot on goal; – players from defending team should attack a player from attacking team who has possessed the ball as quickly as possible, forcing him to act in conditions of time and space deficit; – players should interact with partners quickly; – players should pass the ball to partner timely and precisely, providing him with the time for a shot on goal;

SOCCER. Gaming drills with the contiguous goals for play technique training

Task № 3 continuation

Task description	Requirements for quality of the task execution
Players from the defending team try to prevent players from the attacking team from shooting on goal, acting in the opponent's defending zone. If the goalkeeper from the defending team gets the ball or it's over the goal-line or touchlines from the attacking team players, players from the defending team move to their defending zone for reception of the ball. Corners are not awarded. Offsides are not given. Play time in one repeat is 2 minutes. **Variant:** goals are moved in different directions relative to each other at the goal line 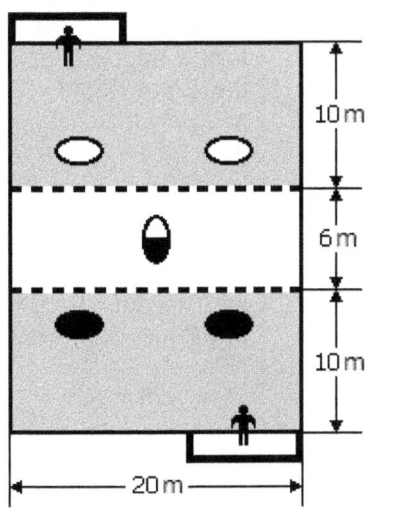	– players should operate with the ball quickly and perform the shooting motion during shots on goal especially fast; – players should shoot on goal from any, even most inconvenient, positions; – during the shots on goal performance players should press for sending the ball into the area of the goal unprotected by the goalkeeper

Task № 4	
Task description	Requirements for quality of the task execution
One on one play with a «neutral» player acting for the attacking team all the time providing shots on goal performance from 16-24 meters after dribbling towards the touchline. There are two zones 12 meters wide and 16 meters long marked on the pitch diagonally to each other. Goals are mounted on opposite short sides of different zones. In each zone goals areas are marked no further than 5 meters from the goal-line, and a «corridor» between zones 24 meters wide and 8 meters long bisected across the width of pitch. Players act in «corridor» all the time. 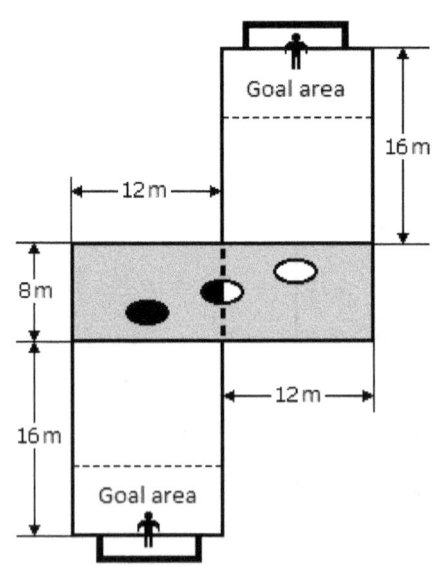	– during the short period of time after a signal for putting the ball into play players should receive the ball from the goalkeeper; – players from the defending team should intercept the ball during the pass performance by the goalkeeper or attack the opponent at the moment of reception of the ball entering into physical contact with him; – players should pass the ball to the partner timely and precisely, providing him with time for delivery of the ball to the opposite half of the «corridor» and shot on goal; – players should receive the ball with an «outgoing»; – receiving the ball players should switch into the game powerfully, moving with it towards the opponent's goal;

SOCCER. Gaming drills with the contiguous goals for play technique training

Task № 4 continuation

Task description	Requirements for quality of the task execution
On a signal goalkeepers put the ball into play from the goal area in the half of the «corridor» situated opposite to their goal, after catching it or when it is out. Players from the attacking team try to deliver the ball to the opposite half of the «corridor» using **dribbling** and shoot on goal in conclusion. Player from the defending team tries to prevent players from the attacking team from delivering the ball to the half of the «corridor» situated opposite to his team goal, and shoot on goal situating during the putting the ball into play by the goalkeeper in the half of the «corridor» situated opposite to the goal of the attacking team. Number of passes by in-field players during the attack is no more than three. If goalkeeper from the defending team gets control over the ball or it is out, player from the defending team and «neutral» player move for reception of the ball away from the goalkeeper to the half of the «corridor» situated opposite to the goal of this team. Corners are not awarded. Offsides are not given. Play time in one repeat – 3 minutes	– players should try to outplay the opponent bravely; – players should operate with the ball quickly and perform the shooting motion during shots on goal especially fast; – players should shoot on goal from any, even most inconvenient, positions with maximum power; – during the shots on goal performance players should press for sending the ball into the area of the goal unprotected by the goalkeeper

Task № 5	
Task description	Requirements for quality of the task execution
One on one play with the «neutral» player acting for the attacking team all the time providing shots on goal performance from 16-24 meters after dribbling towards the goal. Pitch size: 15 meters wide, 40 meters long. There are three zones marked on the pitch: attacking and defensive 16 meters long each, and middle 8 meters long. «Areas of attack beginning» are marked in attacking and defensive zones no further than 10 meters from the goal-line. 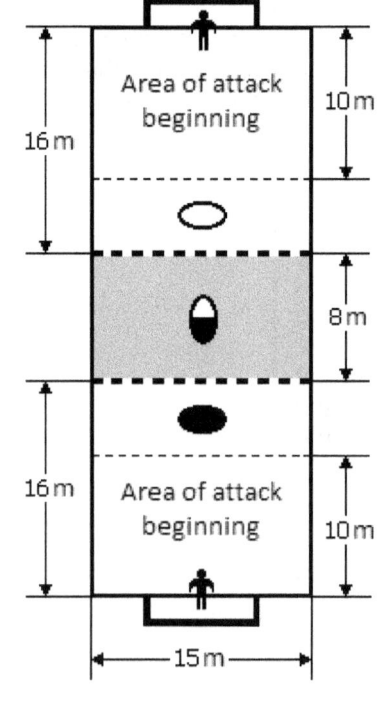	– during the short period of time after a signal for putting the ball into play players should receive the ball from the goalkeeper; – players from the defending team should intercept the ball during the pass performance by the goalkeeper or attack the opponent at the moment of reception of the ball entering into physical contact with him; – players should pass the ball to the partner timely and precisely, providing him with time for delivery of the ball to the middle zone using dribbling and shot on goal; – players should receive the ball with an «outgoing»; – receiving the ball players should switch into the game powerfully, moving with it towards the opponent's goal;

Task № 5 continuation

Task description	Requirements for quality of the task execution
On a signal goalkeepers put the ball into play to their team «area of attack beginning» after catching it or when it is over the goal line and touchlines. Players from the attacking team try to deliver the ball using **dribbling** to the middle zone and shoot on goal in conclusion. Number of passes by in-field players during the attack is no more than two. Player from the defending team tries to prevent players from the attacking team from delivering the ball to the middle zone and shooting on goal, situating in the opponents' «area of attack beginning» when goalkeeper puts the ball into play. If player from the defending team let the ball to cross the touchline, players from the attacking team move for reception of the ball to their team «area of attack beginning». If the goalkeeper from the defending team gets the ball or it's over the goal-line or touchlines from the attacking team players, player from the defending team and «neutral» player move to this team «area of attack beginning» for reception of the ball. Corners are not awarded. Offsides are not given. Play time in one repeat – 3 minutes.	– players should try to outplay the opponent bravely; – players should operate with the ball quickly and perform the shooting motion during shots on goal especially fast; – players should shoot on goal from any, even most inconvenient, positions with maximum power; – during the shots on goal performance players should press for sending the ball into the area of the goal unprotected by the goalkeeper

Task № 5 continuation

Task description	Requirements for quality of the task execution
Variant: one on one play with two «neutral» players one of which acting for the attacking team and another for defending all the time. «Neutral» player acting for the defending team acts only in the middle zone and tries to prevent players from the attacking team from delivering the ball to this zone and shooting on goal	

Section 2. Drills suggesting delivery of the ball in the 18-yard box having used a pass

Task № 1	
Task description	Requirements for quality of the task execution
Two on two play with two «neutral» players acting for the attacking team all the time providing delivery of the ball to the 18-yard box using a pass towards the goal-line. Pitch size: 15 meters wide, 32 meters long. There are three zones marked on the pitch: attacking and defensive 14 meters long each and the middle 4 meters long. «Areas of offside abidance» are marked in defending and attacking zones no further than 8 meters from goal-lines. One player in each team acts in the defensive zone, and another – in the attacking zone all the time. 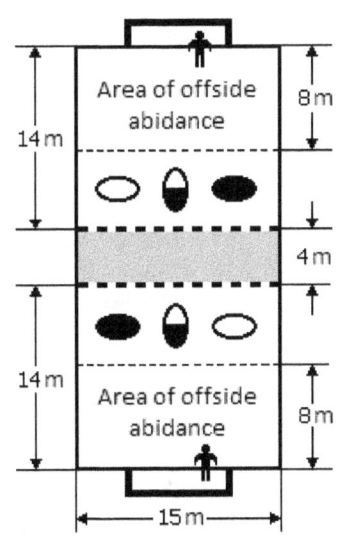	– goalkeepers should put the ball into play without a delay; – player from the defending team should intercept the ball during the pass performance by the goalkeeper or attack the opponent at the moment of reception of the ball entering into physical contact with him; – players from defending team should attack a player from attacking team who has possessed the ball as quickly as possible, forcing him to act in conditions of time and space deficit; – players should pass the ball to the partner into attacking zone timely and precisely; – players should interact with partners quickly;

Task № 1 continuation

Task description	Requirements for quality of the task execution
One «neutral» player acts in the defensive zone of one team, and another – in the defensive zone of another all the time. Players are prohibited from moving from zone to zone. Goalkeepers put the ball into play to the defending zone of their team after catching it of when it is over the goal line and touchlines. Players from the attacking team try to deliver the ball to partners to the attacking zone using passes through the middle zone of the pitch. Number of passes by these players to each other before sending it to the attacking zone is no more than two. Players from the attacking team acting in the attacking zone try to shoot on goal. Number of passes by these layers before shot on goal is no more than one. One player from the attacking team tries to prevent players from the attacking team to deliver the ball to the attacking zone, and another – to shoot on goal. Corners are not awarded. **Offsides are observed in the attacking zone in «area of offside abidance».** Goal scored with a first touch counts as two. Goal scored on the rebound counts as two. Play time in one repeat – 10 minutes.	– players from the attacking team should try to deliver the ball to the attacking zone and shoot on goal quickly; – players from the attacking team located in different zones should act simultaneously in attempts to deliver the ball to the attacking zone; – players should operate with the ball quickly; – players should shoot on goal and execute passes from any, even most inconvenient, positions; – players should shoot on goal and execute passes with a head from any position, even the most inconvenient; – players should press for every opportunity to finish off the ball into the net;

SOCCER. Gaming drills with the contiguous goals for play technique training

Task № 1 continuation

Task description	Requirements for quality of the task execution
Variant: four on four play with two «neutral» players acting for the attacking team all the time. Pitch size: 20 meters wide, 32 meters long. There are three zones marked on the pitch: attacking and defensive 14 meters long each, and the middle 4 meters long. «Areas of offside abidance» are marked in defensive and attacking zones no further than 7 meters from goal-lines. Two players in each team act in the defensive zone and two – in attacking all the time. One «neutral» player acts in the defensive zone of one team, and another in the defensive zone of another team	– during the shots on goal performance players should press for sending the ball into the area of the goal unprotected by the goalkeeper

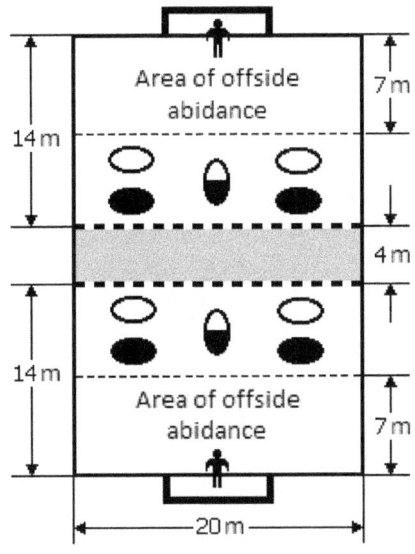

Task № 2	
Task description	Requirements for quality of the task execution
Two on two play with the «neutral» player acting for the attacking team all the time providing delivery of the ball to the 18-yard box using passes towards the goal-line. Pitch size: 12 meters wide, 32 meters long. Middle line of the pitch dividing it into attacking and defensive zones is marked. 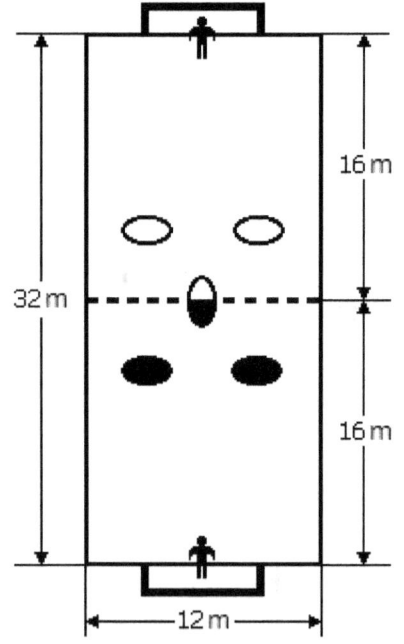 On a signal goalkeepers put the ball into play to their team defending team after catching it or it over the goal-line or touchlines.	– players should receive the ball from the goalkeeper within short period of time after a signal for putting the ball into play; – players from the defending team should intercept the ball during the pass performance by the goalkeeper or attack the opponent at the moment of reception of the ball entering into physical contact with him; – player from the attacking team should open timely for reception of the ball during performance of passes to the attacking team; – players should pass the ball to partner in the attacking zone timely and precisely; – players from the attacking team should try to deliver the ball to the attacking zone and shoot on goal quickly;

SOCCER. Gaming drills with the contiguous goals for play technique training

Task № 2 continuation

Task description	Requirements for quality of the task execution
Players from the attacking team try to deliver the ball to the attacking zone using pass across the middle line only and to shoot on goal from this zone. Number of passes by attacking players in the defending zone before sending the ball across the middle line is no more than three. Number of passes by attacking players in the attacking zone before shot on goal is no more than one. Players from the defending team try to prevent players from the attacking team from delivering the ball to the attacking zone and shooting on goal, positioning in opponents' defending zone during putting the ball into play. Corners are not awarded. **Offsides are given.** Goal scored with a first touch counts as two. Goal scored on the rebound counts as two. Play time in one repeat – 5 minutes. **Variants:** a) three on three play with the «neutral» player acting for the attacking team all the time on the pitch 20 meters wide and 32 meters long; b) goals are moved in different directions relative to each other at the goal line	– players should interact with partners quickly; – players from the defending team should attack a player from attacking team who has possessed the ball as quickly as possible, forcing him to act in conditions of time and space deficit; – players should operate with the ball quickly; – players should shoot on goal from any, even most inconvenient, positions; – players should press for every opportunity to finish off the ball into the net; – during the shots on goal performance players should press for sending the ball into the area of the goal unprotected by the goalkeeper

Task № 3	
Task description	Requirements for quality of the task execution
Four attacking on two defending players play in two zones providing delivery of the ball to the 18-yard box using pass towards the touchline, performed without a peep or during local movements. There are two zones 12 meters wide and 16 meters long opposite one to another with long sides at 14 meters marked on the pitch. Goals are mounted on opposite short sides of different zones. Two attacking and one defending player act in each zone all the time. Players are prohibited from moving from zone to zone. 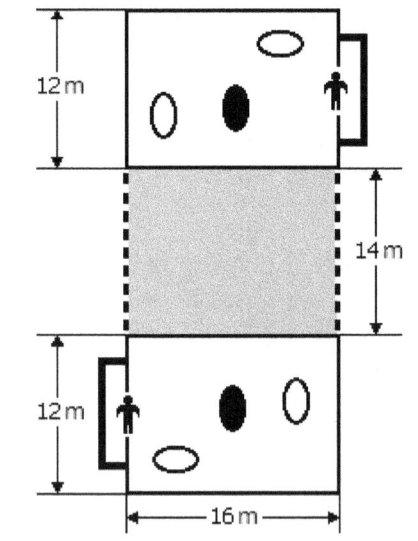	– goalkeepers should put the ball into play without a delay; – defending players should try to intercept balls or attack opponent during the ball reception entering into a physical contact with him; – attacking players acting in one zone should pass the ball to each other timely and precisely, providing partner with time to pass into opposite zone; – players from the defending team should attack a player from attacking team who has possessed the ball as quickly as possible, forcing him to act in conditions of time and space deficit; – attacking players receiving the ball from other zone should try to finish the attack with shot on goal quickly;

Task № 3 continuation

Task description	Requirements for quality of the task execution
Goalkeepers put the ball into play in the zone where the goal they protect is situated after catching it or when it is out of this zone. Two attacking players try to pass the ball to partners in the opposite zone for shooting on goal. Number of passes to each other by attacking players received the ball from the goalkeeper before sending it to the opposite zone is no more than two. Number of passes to each other by attacking players received the ball from the opposite zone before shooting on goal is no more than two. One of defending players tries to prevent attacking players from passing the ball to the opposite zone, and another – to shoot on goal. The task for four attacking players is to score as much goals as possible in a definite time. **Offsides are given.** Goal scored with a first touch counts as two. Goal scored on a rebound counts as two. **Variants:** a) balls are passed from zone to zone with a mounted trajectory so that partner can perform shot on goal or a pass using head; b) zones are marked diagonally to each other	– attacking players located in different zones should act simultaneously in attempts to deliver the ball from zone to zone; – players should operate with the ball quickly; – players should shoot on goal from any position, even the most inconvenient; – players should perform shots on goal and passes with a head including the physical contact with the opponent; – players should try to use every opportunity to finish off the ball into the net; – performing shots on goal players should try to send the ball into goal area unprotected by the goalkeeper

Task № 4	
Task description	Requirements for quality of the task execution
Four attacking players on two defending players in two zones providing delivery of the ball to the 18-yard box using a pass towards the touchline performed during quick movements. There are two zones 12 meters long and 20 meters wide marked on the pitch opposite to each other with long sides at 14 meters. Goal areas are marked in each zone no further than 5 meters from the goal-line. Goals are mounted on opposite short sides of different zones. Two attacking players and one defending player act in each zone all the time. Players are prohibited from moving from zone to zone. 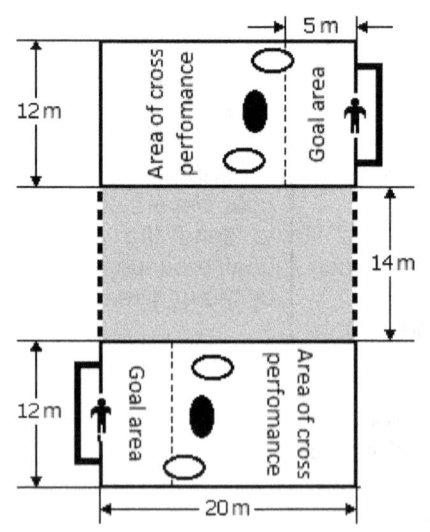	– goalkeepers should put the ball into play without a delay; – players of defending team should intercept the ball during the pass performance by the goalkeeper or attack the opponent at the moment of reception of the ball entering into physical contact with him; – having received the ball from the goalkeeper, attacking players should try to deliver it to the area of performing passes from the flank quickly and pass it to the opposite zone; – players from the defending team should attack a player from attacking team who has possessed the ball as quickly as possible, forcing him to act in conditions of time and space deficit; – attacking players receiving the ball from other zone should try to finish the attack with shot on goal quickly;

Task № 4 continuation

Task description	Requirements for quality of the task execution
Goalkeepers put the ball into play into the goal area after catching it or when it is out of this zone. Two attacking players try to deliver the ball to the «area of cross performing» and pass it into the opposite zone to partners for shot on goal. Number of passes to each other by attacking players received the ball from the goalkeeper before sending it to the opposite zone is no more than two. Number of passes to each other by attacking players received the ball from the opposite zone before shot on goal is no more than two. One of attacking players tries to prevent attacking players from passing to the opposite zone, and the other – to shoot on goal. While goalkeeper puts the ball into play defending player acting in this zone stands in goal area. Task for four attacking players is to score as much goals as possible in definite time. **Offsides are given.** Goal scored with a first touch counts as two. Goal scored at the rebound counts as two. **Variant:** balls are passed from zone to zone with a mounted trajectory so that partner can perform shot on goal or a pass using head	– attacking players located in different zones should act simultaneously in attempts to deliver the ball from zone to zone; – players should operate with the ball quickly; – players should shoot on goal from any, even most inconvenient, positions; – players should perform shots on goal and passes with a head including the physical contact with the opponent; – players should press for every opportunity to finish off the ball into the net; – during the shots on goal performance players should press for sending the ball into the area of the goal unprotected by the goalkeeper

Section 3. Drills suggesting delivery of the ball to the 18-yard box using dribbling

Task № 1	
Task description	Requirements for quality of the task execution
One on one play with the «neutral» player acting for the attacking team all the time providing delivery of the ball to the 18-yard box using dribbling towards the goal-line. Pitch size: 12 meters wide, 32 meters long. Half-way line which divides pitch into attacking and defensive zones is marked. Attacking and defensive zone are divided in two. 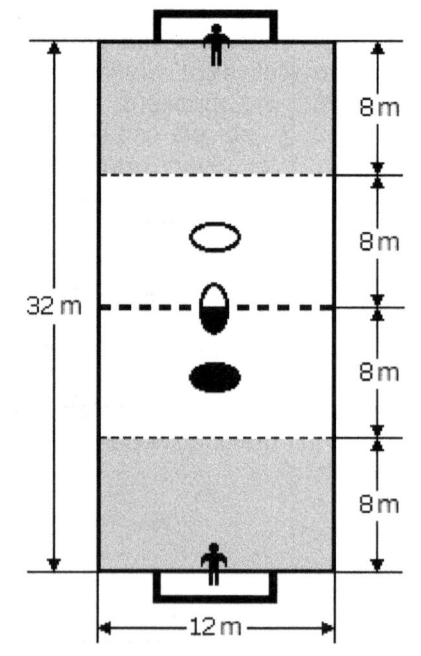	– players should receive the ball from the goalkeeper within short period of time after a signal for putting the ball into play; – player from the defending team should intercept the ball during the pass performance by the goalkeeper or attack the opponent at the moment of reception of the ball entering into physical contact with him; – players should pass the ball to the partner timely and precisely, providing him with time for delivery of the ball to the attacking zone and shot on goal; – players should receive the ball with an «outgoing»; – players from the attacking team should try to deliver the ball to the attacking zone and shoot on goal quickly;

Task № 1 continuation

Task description	Requirements for quality of the task execution
On a signal goalkeepers put the ball into play to the middle zone from the goal area after catching it or when it is over the goal line and touchlines. Players from the attacking team try to deliver the ball to nearest relative to the midline of the pitch half of the attacking zone using dribbling and shoot on goal in conclusion. Number of passes by attacking players in the defending zone before crossing the midline is no more than two. Player from the defending team tries to prevent players from the attacking team from delivering the ball to the attacking zone and shooting on goal, locating in opponent's defending zone during putting the ball into play. Corners are not awarded. **Offsides are given.** Goal scored at the rebound counts as two. Play time in one repeat – 5 minutes. **Variants:** a) two on two play with the «neutral» player acting for the attacking team all the time at the pitch 20 meters wide and 32 meters long; b) three on three play with the «neutral» player acting for the attacking team all the time at the pitch 25 meters wide and 32 meters long; c) goals are moved in different directions relative to each other at the goal line	– receiving the ball players should switch into the game powerfully, moving with it towards the opponent's goal; – players should cross the midline with the ball including outplaying an opponent; – players should operate with the ball quickly; – players should shoot on goal from any, even most inconvenient, positions; – players should press for every opportunity to finish off the ball into the net; – during the shots on goal performance players should press for sending the ball into the area of the goal unprotected by the goalkeeper

Task № 2

Task description	Requirements for quality of the task execution
One on one play with two «neutral» players, one of which acts for the attacking team, and another – for the defending, providing delivery of the ball to the 18-yard box using dribbling towards the goal-line. Pitch size: 12 meters wide, 32 meters long. There are three zones marked on the pitch: attacking and defending 15 meters long, and the middle 2 meters long. «Neutral» player acting for the defending team all the time acts in the middle zone only. 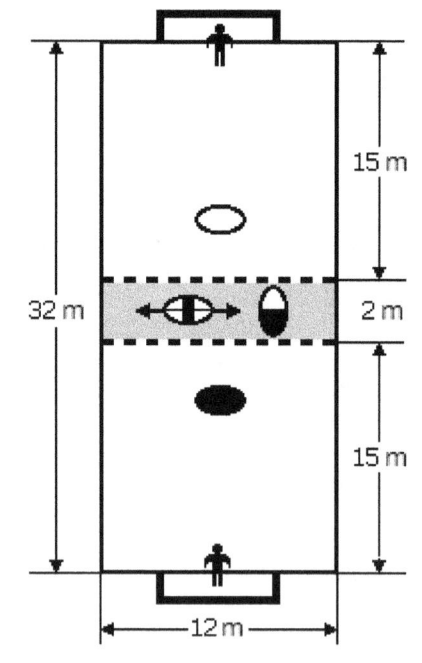	– players should receive the ball from the goalkeeper within short period of time after a signal for putting the ball into play; – player from the defending team should intercept the ball during the pass performance by the goalkeeper or attack the opponent at the moment of reception of the ball entering into physical contact with him; – players should pass the ball to partner timely and accurately, giving him time for performance of shot on goal; – players should receive the ball with an «outgoing»; – players should try to deliver the ball to the attacking zone and shoot on goal quickly;

SOCCER. Gaming drills with the contiguous goals for play technique training

Task № 2 continuation

Task description	Requirements for quality of the task execution
On a signal goalkeepers put the ball into play to their team defending zone after catching it or when it is over the goal-line and touchlines. Players from the attacking team try to deliver the ball to the attacking zone using dribbling and shoot on goal in conclusion. Number of passes by attacking players in the defending zone before crossing the middle zone is no more than three. Player from the defending team tries to prevent players from the attacking team from delivering the ball to the attacking zone and shooting on goal, situating in opponents' defending zone during putting the ball into play. «Neutral» player acting for the defending team all the time tries to prevent players from the attacking team from delivering the ball to the attacking zone. Corners are not awarded. **Offsides are given.** Goal scored at the rebound counts as two. Play time in one repeat – 5 minutes. **Variants:** a) two on two play with two «neutral» players, one of which acts for the attacking team, and the other for the defending, on the pitch 20 meters wide and 32 meters long; b) goals are moved in different directions relative to each other at the goal-line	– receiving the ball players should switch into the game powerfully, moving with it towards the goal; – players should cross the midline with the ball including outplaying an opponent; – players should operate with the ball quickly; – players should shoot on goal from any, even most inconvenient, positions; – players should press for every opportunity to finish off the ball into the net; – during the shots on goal performance players should press for sending the ball into the area of the goal unprotected by the goalkeeper

Task № 3	
Task description	Requirements for quality of the task execution
One on one play with the «neutral» player acting for the attacking team all the time providing delivery of the ball to the 18-yard box using dribbling towards the touchline. Pitch size: 30 meters wide, 16 meters long. There are three zones marked on the pitch: two lateral 7 meters wide and the middle 16 meters wide. Goals are moved in different directions relative to each other at the goal-line and mounted near pitch corners. 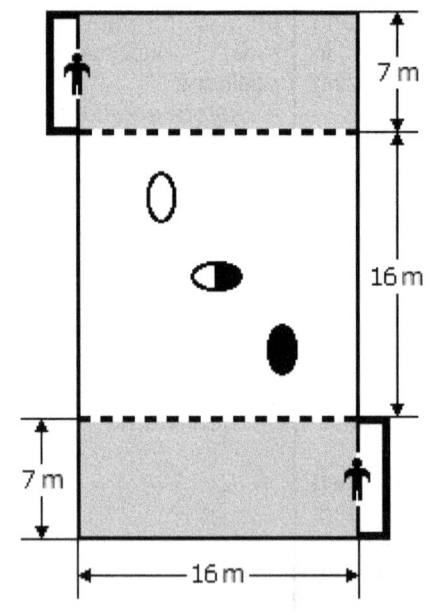	– players should receive the ball from the goalkeeper within short period of time after a signal for putting the ball into play; – player from the defending team should intercept the ball during the pass performance by the goalkeeper or attack the opponent at the moment of reception of the ball entering into physical contact with him; – players should pass the ball to the partner timely and precisely, providing him with time for delivery of the ball to the middle zone and shooting on goal; – players should operate with the ball quickly; – players should try to deliver the ball to the middle zone quickly and shoot on goal; – players should receive the ball with an «outgoing»;

Task № 3 continuation

Task description	Requirements for quality of the task execution
On a signal goalkeepers put the ball into play to their team lateral zone after catching it or when it is over the goal-line and touchlines. Players from the attacking team try to deliver the ball to the middle zone using dribbling and shoot on goal in conclusion. Number of passes by attacking players in their lateral zone before moving to the middle zone is no more than two. Player from the defending team tries to prevent players from the attacking team from delivering the ball to the middle zone and shooting on goal, situating in the opponents' lateral zone during putting the ball into play. Players are permitted to shoot on goal from the opponents' lateral zone. Corners are not awarded. Offsides are not given. Goal scored at the rebound counts as two. Play time in one repeat – 5 minutes. **Variant:** two on two play with the «neutral» player acting for the attacking team all the time. Pitch size: 40 meters wide, 16 meters long. Width of lateral zones is 12 meters, middle zone – 16 meters. Goals are mounted 5 meters away from the corners of the pitch	– receiving the ball players should switch into the game powerfully, moving with it towards the opponent's goal; – players should cross the midline with the ball including outplaying an opponent; – players should shoot on goal from any, even most inconvenient, positions; – players should press for every opportunity to finish off the ball into the net; – during the shots on goal performance players should press for sending the ball into the area of the goal unprotected by the goalkeeper

Task № 4	
Task description	Requirements for quality of the task execution
One on one play with two «neutral» players, one of which acts for the attacking team, and another – for the defending team all the time, providing delivery of the ball to the 18-yard box using dribbling towards the touchline. Pitch size: 30 meters wide, 16 meters long. There are three zones marked on the pitch: two lateral 7 meters wide each, and the middle 16 meters wide. Goals are moved in different directions relative to each other at the goal-line and mounted near pitch corners. «Neutral» player acting for the defending team all the time acts in the middle zone only. 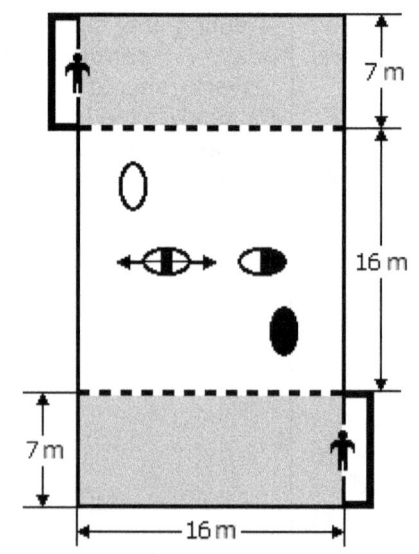	– players should receive the ball from the goalkeeper within short period of time after a signal for putting the ball into play; – player from the defending team should intercept the ball during the pass performance by the goalkeeper or attack the opponent at the moment of reception of the ball entering into physical contact with him; – players should pass the ball to partner timely and accurately, giving him time for delivery of the ball to the middle zone and shooting on goal; – players should operate with the ball quickly; – players should try to deliver the ball to the middle zone quickly and shoot on goal; – players should receive the ball with an «outgoing»;

Task № 4 continuation

Task description	Requirements for quality of the task execution
On a signal goalkeepers put the ball into play to their team lateral zone after catching it or when it is over the goal-line and touchlines. Players from the attacking team try to deliver the ball to the middle zone using dribbling and shoot on goal in conclusion. Number of passes by attacking players in their lateral zone before moving to the middle zone is no more than three. Player from the defending team tries to prevent players from the attacking team from delivering the ball to the middle zone and shooting on goal, situating in the opponents' lateral zone during putting the ball into play. «Neutral» player acting for the defending team all the time tries to prevent players from the attacking team from delivering the ball to the middle zone and shooting on goal. Players are permitted to shoot on goal from the opponents' lateral zone. Corners are not awarded. Offsides are not given. Goal scored at the rebound counts as two. Play time in one repeat – 5 minutes	– receiving the ball players should switch into the game powerfully, moving with it towards the touchline; – players should move to the middle zone with the ball including outplaying the opponent; – players should shoot on goal from any, even most inconvenient, positions; – players should press for every opportunity to finish off the ball into the net a; – during the shots on goal performance players should press for sending the ball into the area of the goal unprotected by the goalkeeper

Section 4. Drills suggesting delivery of the ball to the 18-yard box using dribbling or a pass depending on situation

Task № 1	
Task description	Requirements for quality of the task execution
Two on two play with the «neutral» player acting for the attacking team all the time providing delivery of the ball into the 18-yard box using dribbling or a pass towards the goal-line depending on situation. Pitch size: 12 meters wide, 32 meters long. Half-way line which divides pitch into attacking and defensive zones is marked. 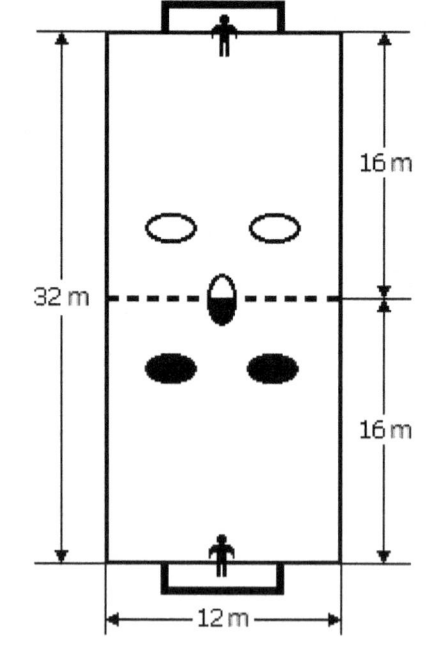	– players should receive the ball from the goalkeeper within short period of time after a signal for putting the ball into play; – players from the defending team should intercept the ball during the pass performance by the goalkeeper or attack the opponent at the moment of reception of the ball entering into physical contact with him; – players should try to deliver the ball to the attacking zone quickly and shoot on goal; – players from the attacking team should open timely for reception of the ball during performance of passes to the attacking zone; – players should receive the ball with the «outgoing»;

SOCCER. Gaming drills with the contiguous goals for play technique training

Task № 1 continuation

Task description	Requirements for quality of the task execution
On a signal goalkeepers put the ball into play to their team lateral zone after catching it or when it is over the goal-line and touchlines. Players from the attacking team try to deliver the ball to the attacking zone using dribbling or a pass depending on situation and shoot on goal from this zone. Number of passes by attacking players in the defending zone before crossing the midline is no more than two. Number of passes by attacking players in the attacking zone before shot on goal is no more than one. Players from the defending team try to prevent players from the attacking team from delivering the ball to the attacking zone and shooting on goal, positioning in opponents' defending zone during putting the ball into play. Corners are not awarded. **Offsides are given.** Goal scored with a first touch counts as two. Goal scored at the rebound counts as two. Play time in one repeat – 5 minutes. **Variants:** a) three on three play with the «neutral» player acting for the attacking team all the time, on the pitch 20 meters wide and 32 long; b) goals are moved in different directions relative to each other at the goal-line	– players should cross the midline with the ball including outplaying an opponent; – players from the defending team should attack a player from the attacking team who has possessed the ball as quickly as possible, forcing him to act in conditions of time and space deficit; – players should operate with the ball quickly; – players should shoot on goal from any, even most inconvenient, positions; – players should press for every opportunity to finish off the ball into the net; – during the shots on goal performance players should press for sending the ball into the area of the goal unprotected by the goalkeeper

Task № 2	
Task description	Requirements for quality of the task execution
Two on two play providing delivery of the ball to the 18-yard box using dribbling or a pass towards the goal depending on situation. Pitch size: 12 meters wide, 32 meters long. Half-way line which divides pitch into attacking and defensive zones is marked. 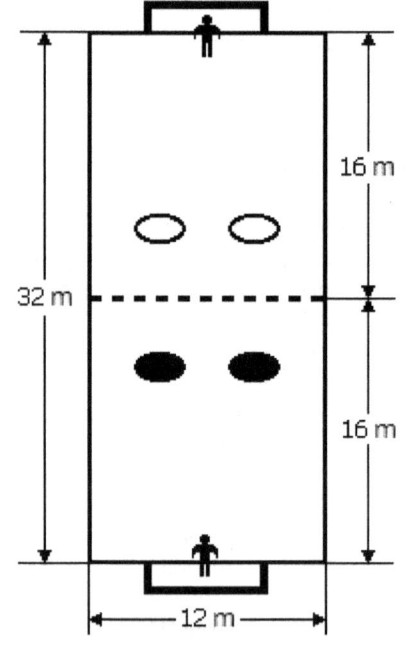 On a signal goalkeepers put the ball into play to their team lateral zone after catching it or when it is over the goal-line and touchlines.	– players should receive the ball from the goalkeeper within short period of time after a signal for putting the ball into play; – players from the defending team should intercept the ball during the pass performance by the goalkeeper or attack the opponent at the moment of reception of the ball entering into physical contact with him; – players should try to deliver the ball to the attacking zone quickly and shoot on goal; – players from the attacking team should open timely for reception of the ball during performance of passes to the attacking zone; – players should receive the ball with the «outgoing»; – players should operate with the ball quickly;

SOCCER. Gaming drills with the contiguous goals for play technique training

Task № 2 continuation

Task description	Requirements for quality of the task execution
Players from the attacking team try to deliver the ball to the attacking zone using dribbling or a pass depending on situation and shoot on goal from this zone. Number of passes by attacking players in the defending zone before crossing the midline is no more than two. Number of passes by attacking players in the attacking zone before shot on goal is no more than one. Players from the defending team try to prevent players from the attacking team from delivering the ball to the attacking zone and shooting on goal, positioning in opponents' defending zone during putting the ball into play. Corners are not awarded. **Offsides are given.** Goal scored with a first touch counts as two. Goal scored at the rebound counts as two. Play time in one repeat – 5 minutes. **Variants:** a) three on three play on the pitch 20 meters wide and 32 meters long; b) four on four play on the pitch 25 meters wide and 32 meters long; c) goals are moved in different directions relative to each other at the goal-line	– players should cross the midline with the ball including outplaying an opponent; – players from the defending team should attack a player from the attacking team who has possessed the ball as quickly as possible, forcing him to act in conditions of time and space deficit; – players should shoot on goal from any, even most inconvenient, positions; – players should press for every opportunity to finish off the ball into the net; – during the shots on goal performance players should press for sending the ball into the area of the goal unprotected by the goalkeeper

Task № 3	
Task description	Requirements for quality of the task execution
One on one play with two «neutral» players, one of which acts for the attacking team, and the other – for the defending all the time, providing delivery of the ball to the 18-yard box using dribbling or a pass towards the goal-line depending on situation. Pitch size: 12 meters wide, 32 meters long. There are three zones marked on the pitch: attacking and defending 14 meters long each, and the middle 4 meters long. «Neutral» player acting for the defending team all the time acts only in the middle zone. 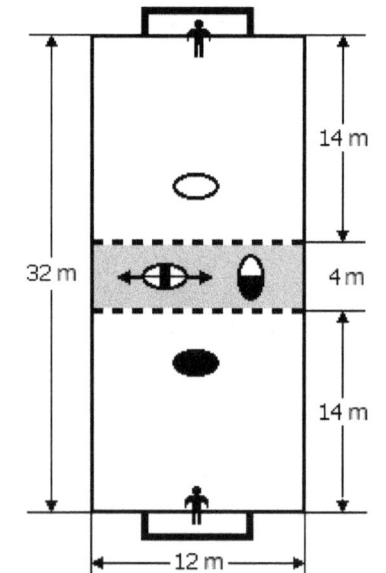	– players should receive the ball from the goalkeeper within short period of time after a signal for putting the ball into play; – players from the defending team should intercept the ball during the pass performance by the goalkeeper or attack the opponent at the moment of reception of the ball entering into physical contact with him; – players should try to deliver the ball to the attacking zone quickly and shoot on goal; – players from the attacking team should open timely for reception of the ball during performance of passes to the attacking zone; – players should receive the ball with the «outgoing»; – players should operate with the ball quickly;

Task № 3 continuation

Task description	Requirements for quality of the task execution
On a signal goalkeepers put the ball into play to their team lateral zone after catching it or when it is over the goal-line and touchlines. Players from the attacking team try to deliver the ball to the attacking zone using dribbling or a pass depending on situation and shoot on goal from this zone. Number of passes by attacking players in the defending zone before crossing the midline is no more than three. Number of passes by attacking players in the attacking zone before shot on goal is no more than one. Player from the defending team tries to prevent players from the attacking team from delivering the ball to the attacking zone and shooting on goal, positioning in opponents' defending zone during putting the ball into play. «Neutral» player acting for the defending team all the time tries to prevent players from the attacking team to deliver the ball to the attacking zone. Corners are not awarded. **Offsides are given in the attacking zone.** Goal scored with a first touch counts as two. Goal scored at the rebound counts as two. Play time in one repeat – 5 minutes.	– players should cross the midline with the ball including outplaying an opponent; – players from the defending team should attack a player from the attacking team who has possessed the ball as quickly as possible, forcing him to act in conditions of time and space deficit; – players should shoot on goal from any, even most inconvenient, positions; – players should press for every opportunity to finish off the ball into the net; – during the shots on goal performance players should press for sending the ball into the area of the goal unprotected by the goalkeeper

Task № 3 continuation

Task description	Requirements for quality of the task execution
Variants: a) two on two play with two «neutral» players, one of which acts for the attacking team, and the other – for the defending all the time, on the pitch 20 meters wide and 32 meters long; b) three on three play with two «neutral» players, one of which acts for the attacking team, and the other – for the defending all the time, on the pitch 25 meters long and 32 meters long; c) goals are moved in different directions relative to each other at the goal-line	

SOCCER. Gaming drills with the contiguous goals for play technique training

Task № 4	
Task description	Requirements for quality of the task execution
Three on three play with the «neutral» player acting for the attacking team all the time, providing delivery of the ball to the 18-yard box using dribbling or a pass towards the touchline depending on situation. Pitch size: 30 meters wide, 16 meters long. There are three zones marked on the pitch: two lateral 7 meters wide each, and the middle 16 meters wide. Goals are moved in different directions relative to each other at the goal-line and mounted by the corners of the pitch. 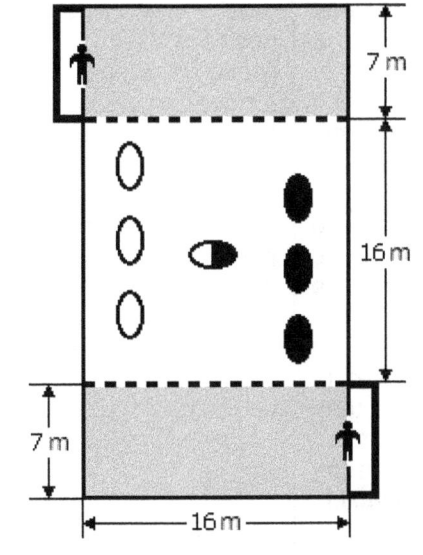	– players should receive the ball from the goalkeeper within short period of time after a signal for putting the ball into play; – players from the defending team should intercept the ball during the pass performance by the goalkeeper or attack the opponent at the moment of reception of the ball entering into physical contact with him; – players should try to deliver the ball to the middle zone quickly and shoot on goal; – players from the attacking team should open timely for reception of the ball during performance of passes to the middle zone; – players should receive the ball with the «outgoing»; – players should operate with the ball quickly;

Task № 4 continuation

Task description	Requirements for quality of the task execution
On a signal goalkeepers put the ball into play to their team lateral zone after catching it or when it is over the goal-line and touchlines. During putting the ball into play players are located in such a manner: – one player from the attacking team, one player from the defending team and the «neutral» player in the attacking team lateral zone; – two players from the attacking team and two players from the attacking team in the middle zone. Players from the attacking team receiving the ball from the goalkeeper in their team lateral zone try to deliver the ball to the middle zone using dribbling or passes depending on situation and shoot on goal or make a pass to the partner for shooting on goal from this zone. Number of passes by attacking players in their team lateral zone before delivery of the ball to the middle zone is no more than two. Number of passes by attacking players in the middle zone before shooting on goal is no more than two. Players from the defending team try to prevent player from the attacking team from delivery of the ball to the middle zone and shooting on goal. Players are permitted to shoot on goal from the opponent's lateral zone.	– players should cross the midline with the ball including outplaying an opponent; – players from the defending team should attack a player from the attacking team who has possessed the ball as quickly as possible, forcing him to act in conditions of time and space deficit; – players should shoot on goal from any, even most inconvenient, positions; – players should press for every opportunity to finish off the ball into the net; – during the shots on goal performance players should press for sending the ball into the area of the goal unprotected by the goalkeeper

SOCCER. Gaming drills with the contiguous goals for play technique training

Task № 4 continuation

Task description	Requirements for quality of the task execution
Corners are not awarded. **Offsides are given.** Goal scored with the first touch counts as two. Goal scored at the rebound counts as two. Play time in one repeat – 5 minutes. **Variant:** two on two play with two «neutral» players, one of which acts for the attacking team, and another – for the defending all the time. «Neutral» player acting for the defending team all the time acts in the middle zone only. 7 m 16 m 7 m 16 m	

Task № 5	
Task description	Requirements for quality of the task execution
Two on two play with the «neutral» player acting for the attacking team all the time providing delivery of the ball to the 18-yard box using dribbling or a pass towards the touchline depending on situation. Pitch size: 36 meters wide, 16 meters wide. There are three zones marked on the pitch: two lateral 10 meters wide each, and the middle 16 meters wide. Goals are moved in different directions relative to each other at the goal-line and mounted 3 meters away from corners of the pitch. 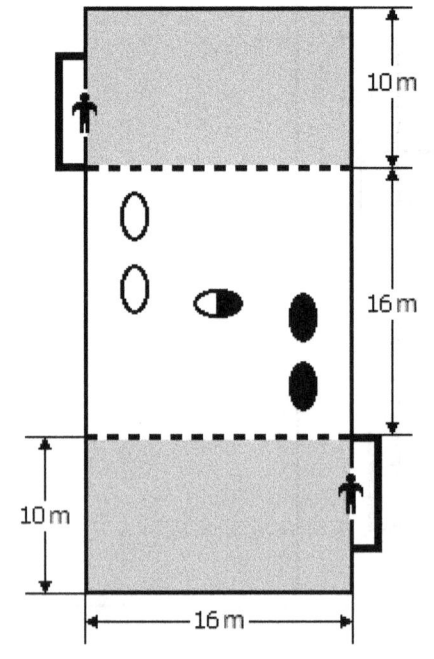	– players should receive the ball from the goalkeeper within short period of time after a signal for putting the ball into play; – players from the defending team should intercept the ball during the pass performance by the goalkeeper or attack the opponent at the moment of reception of the ball entering into physical contact with him; – players should try to deliver the ball to the middle zone quickly and shoot on goal; – players from the attacking team should open timely for reception of the ball during performance of passes to the middle zone; – players should receive the ball with the «outgoing»; – players should operate with the ball quickly;

Task № 5 continuation

Task description	Requirements for quality of the task execution
On a signal goalkeepers put the ball into play to their team lateral zone after catching it or when it is over the goal-line and touchlines. During putting the ball into play all the players are situated in the attacking team lateral zone. Players from the attacking team try to deliver the ball to the middle zone using dribbling or a pass depending on situation and shoot on goal from this zone. Number of passes by attacking players in their team lateral zone before delivering the ball to the middle zone is no more than two. Players from the defending team try to prevent players from the attacking team from delivering the ball to the middle zone and shooting on goal. Players are permitted to shoot on goal from the opponent's lateral zone. Corners are not awarded. **Offsides are given**. Goal scored at the rebound counts as two. Play time in one repeat – 5 minutes. **Variant:** three on three play with the «neutral» player acting for the attacking team all the time. Pitch size: 40 meters wide, 16 meters long. Width of lateral zones – 12 meters, middle zone – 16 meters. Goals are mounted 5 meters away from corners of the pitch	– players should cross the midline with the ball including outplaying an opponent; – players from the defending team should attack a player from the attacking team who has possessed the ball as quickly as possible, forcing him to act in conditions of time and space deficit; – players should shoot on goal from any, even most inconvenient, positions; – players should press for every opportunity to finish off the ball into the net; – during the shots on goal performance players should press for sending the ball into the area of the goal unprotected by the goalkeeper

Task № 6	
Task description	Requirements for quality of the task execution
Three on three play providing delivery of the ball to the 18-yard box using dribbling or a pass towards the touchline depending on situation. Pitch size: 30 meters wide, 16 meters long. There are three zones marked on the pitch: two lateral 7 meters wide each, and the middle 16 meters wide. Goals are moved in different directions relative to each other at the goal-line and mounted at corners of the pitch. 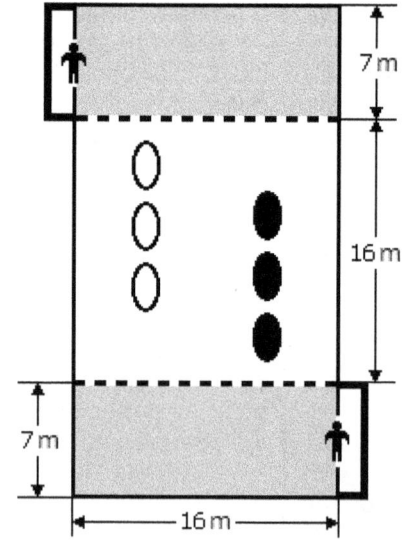 On a signal goalkeepers put the ball into play to their team lateral zone after catching it or when it is over the goal-line and touchlines.	– players should receive the ball from the goalkeeper within short period of time after a signal for putting the ball into play; – players from the defending team should intercept the ball during the pass performance by the goalkeeper or attack the opponent at the moment of reception of the ball entering into physical contact with him; – players should try to deliver the ball to the middle zone quickly and shoot on goal; – players from the attacking team should open timely for reception of the ball during performance of passes to the middle zone; – players should receive the ball with the «outgoing»; – players should operate with the ball quickly;

SOCCER. Gaming drills with the contiguous goals for play technique training

Task № 6 continuation

Task description	Requirements for quality of the task execution
During putting the ball into play players are situated in such a manner: – one player from the attacking team and one player from the defending team in attacking team lateral zone; – two players from the attacking team and two players from the defending team in the middle zone. Player from the attacking team receiving the ball from the goalkeeper in his team lateral zone tries to deliver the ball to the middle zone using dribbling or a pass depending on situation and shoot on goal or make a pass to partners for shooting on goal from this zone. Number of passes by attacking players in the middle zone before shooting on goal is no more than two. Players from the defending team tries to prevent players from the attacking team from delivering the ball to the middle zone and shooting on goal. Players are permitted to shoot on goal from the opponent's lateral zone. Corners are not awarded. **Offsides are given.** Goal scored with the first touch counts as two. Goal scored at the rebound counts as two. Play time in one repeat – 5 minutes	– players should cross the midline with the ball including outplaying an opponent; – players from the defending team should attack a player from the attacking team who has possessed the ball as quickly as possible, forcing him to act in conditions of time and space deficit; – players should shoot on goal from any, even most inconvenient, positions; – players should press for every opportunity to finish off the ball into the net; – during the shots on goal performance players should press for sending the ball into the area of the goal unprotected by the goalkeeper

CHAPTER IV.
GAMING DRILLS WITH THE CONTIGUOUS GOALS FOR PLAY TECHNIQUE TRAINING IN THE MIDFIELD ZONE

4. 1. Drills elaboration

The following have been considered during elaboration of gaming drills with the contiguous goals for play technique training in the midfield zone.

First. Delivery of the ball forward in the midfield zone and from the middle zone to the attacking zone is performed using dribbling and passes on various distance, performed both separately and in combination.

Second. In contrast to play situation in the attacking zone, in which footballers are challenged for quick and right decision-making on beginning of attacking actions after taking possession of the ball foremost, in game episodes in the midfield zone the quickness of ball passing the space towards the opponent's goal-line comes to the fore.

Third. The quickness of passing the space by the ball may be achieved if players act on the relay race principle: after taking possession of the ball move with it quickly towards the opponent's goal-line and pass the ball to the partner who will also quickly move with the ball forward.

Fourth. While overcrowding at relatively small section of the pitch the successive space passing may be accomplished with several short passes performed «in two quick touches», when combination of actions «reception and passing of the ball» is performed with the same leg, and the second touch of the ball follows the first without a delay.

In these cases time spent on passes performance is not much more than while passing the ball with the first touch, whereas the precision of sending the ball is higher, and furthermore players may change the direction of the pass or retreat from it if necessary.

Fifth. While delivering the ball forward using passes on medium and long distance players are required to have the ability to receive the ball, sent with sufficient high speed, in conditions of opponency with the following continuation of attacking actions.

Taking possession of the ball in such situations may be performed with the back to the defending team goal (in static position or with outing to the ball) and after moving to the ball at different angles relatively to the goal-line.

With account of specifics of attacking actions technique in the midfield zone in competitive games and regularities of fitness transition in precision and speed of actions with the ball there are three sections of gaming drills with the contiguous goals for play technique training in the midfield zone (fig. 13).

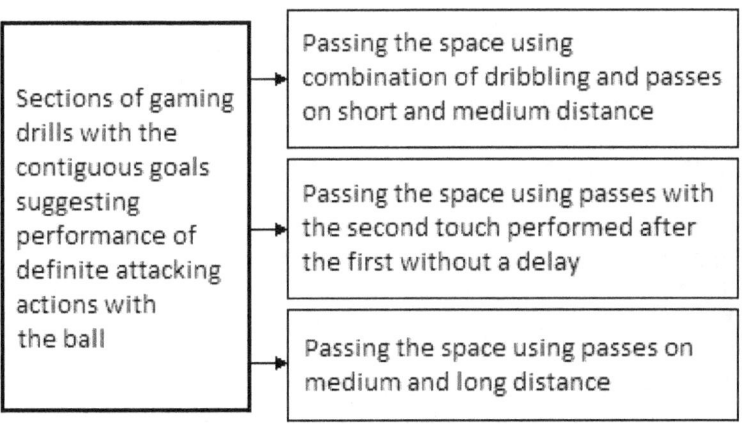

Fig. 13. Section of gaming drills with the contiguous goals for play technique training in the midfield zone

4. 2. Drills examples

Section 1. Drills suggesting passing the space using combination of dribbling and passes on short and medium distance

Task № 1	
Task description	Requirements for quality of the task execution
One on one play with four «neutral» players, two of which act for the attacking team, and other two – for the defending, providing passing the space using dribbling and passes on short and medium distance. Pitch size: 15 meters wide, 50 meters long. There are three zones marked on the pitch: attacking and defending 15 meters long each, and the middle 20 meters long. Middle zone is divided in two along the length of the pitch. Two «neutral» players acting for the defending team all the time act in the middle zone only: one in one half of this zone, and another in another half. On a signal goalkeepers put the ball into play to their team lateral zone after catching it or when it is over the goal-line and touchlines. Players from the attacking team try to deliver the ball to the attacking zone as fast as possible, using combination of dribbling and passes, and shoot on goal from this zone.	– players should receive the ball from the goalkeeper within short period of time after a signal for putting the ball into play; – players from the defending team should intercept the ball during the pass performance by the goalkeeper or attack the opponent at the moment of reception of the ball entering into physical contact with him; – players should try to deliver the ball to the middle zone quickly and shoot on goal; – players should send the ball to each other so that it should be comfortable to receive without slowing down;

Task № 1 continuation

Task description	Requirements for quality of the task execution
(diagram: field 50 m long, 15 m wide, with zones of 15 m, 10 m, 10 m, 15 m)	– players should cross the midline with the ball including outplaying an opponent; – attacking players should slow down while outplaying an opponent as low as possible; – players from the defending team should attack a player from the attacking team who has possessed the ball as quickly as possible, forcing him to act in conditions of time and space deficit; – players should operate with the ball quickly; – players should shoot on goal from any, even most inconvenient, positions; – players should press for every opportunity to finish off the ball into the net; – during the shots on goal performance players should press for sending the ball into the area of the goal unprotected by the goalkeeper
Player from the defending team tries to prevent players from the attacking team from delivering the ball to the attacking zone and shooting on goal, situating in the opponent's defending zone during putting the ball into play. Two «neutral» players acting for the defending team all the time try to prevent players from the attacking team from delivering the ball to the attacking zone.	

Task № 1 continuation

Task description	Requirements for quality of the task execution
Corners are not awarded. **Offsides are given in the attacking zone.** Goal scored with a first touch counts as two. Goal scored at the rebound counts as two. Play time in one repeat – 5 minutes. **Variant:** two on two play with four «neutral» players, two of which act for the attacking team, and another two – for the defending all the time, on the pitch 20 meters wide and 50 meters long	

Task № 2	
Task description	Requirements for quality of the task execution
One on one play with three «neutral» players, two of which act for the attacking team, and another – for the defending all the time, providing passing the space using dribbling and passes on short and medium distance. Pitch size: 15 meters wide, 30 meters long. There are three zones marked on the pitch: attacking and defending 12 meters long each, and the middle 6 meters long. One of «neutral» players acting for the attacking team all the time, and «neutral» player acting for the defending team act in the midfield zone only. 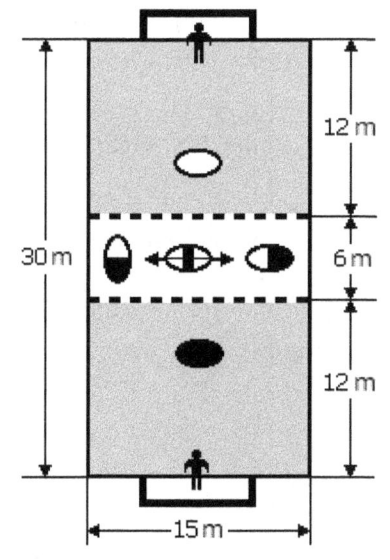	– players should receive the ball from the goalkeeper within short period of time after a signal for putting the ball into play; – players from the defending team should intercept the ball during the pass performance by the goalkeeper or attack the opponent at the moment of reception of the ball entering into physical contact with him; – players should try to deliver the ball to the attacking zone quickly and shoot on goal; – players should send the ball to each other so that it should be comfortable to receive without slowing down; – players should cross the midline with the ball including outplaying an opponent; – attacking players should slow down while outplaying an opponent as low as possible;

Task № 2 continuation

Task description	Requirements for quality of the task execution
On a signal goalkeepers put the ball into play to their team lateral zone after catching it or when it is over the goal-line and touchlines. Players from the attacking team try to deliver the ball to the attacking zone as fast as possible, using combination of dribbling and passes and shoot on goal from this zone. Players from the attacking zone are permitted to pass the ball to the «neutral» player, acting for the attacking team all the time and in the midfield zone, at any point, and receive the ball from him at any place of the pitch. Player from the defending team tries to prevent players from the attacking team to deliver the ball to the attacking zone and shoot on goal, situating in the opponent's defending zone during putting the ball into play. «Neutral» player acting for the defending team tries to prevent players from the attacking team to deliver the ball to the attacking zone. Corners are not awarded. **Offsides are given in the attacking zone.** Goal scored with a first touch counts as two. Goal scored at the rebound counts as two. Play time in one repeat – 5 minutes.	– players from the defending team should attack a player from the attacking team who has possessed the ball as quickly as possible, forcing him to act in conditions of time and space deficit; – players should operate with the ball quickly; – players should shoot on goal from any, even most inconvenient, positions; – players should press for every opportunity to finish off the ball into the net; – during the shots on goal performance players should press for sending the ball into the area of the goal unprotected by the goalkeeper

SOCCER. Gaming drills with the contiguous goals for play technique training

Task № 2 continuation

Task description	Requirements for quality of the task execution
Variant: two on two play with three «neutral» players, two of which act for the attacking team, and one – for the defending all the time, on the pitch 20 meters wide and 30 meters long. One of «neutral» players acting for the attacking team all the time, and «neutral» player acting for the defending team all the time, act in the midfield zone only. 30 m / 20 m / 12 m / 6 m / 12 m	

Section 2. Drills suggesting passing the space using passes with the second touch performed after the first without a delay

Task № 1	
Task description	Requirements for quality of the task execution
Two on two play with two «neutral» players acting for the attacking team all the time providing passing the space using passes with the second touch performed after the first without a delay. Pitch size: 15 meters wide, 30 meters long. Half-way line which divides pitch into attacking and defensive zones is marked. 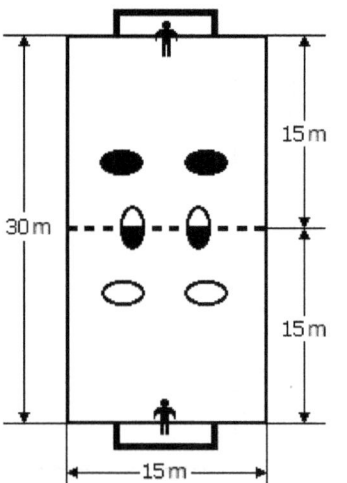 On a signal goalkeepers put the ball into play to their team defending zone after catching it or when it is over the goal-line and touchlines.	– goalkeepers should put the ball into play without a delay; – players from the defending team should intercept the ball during the pass performance by the goalkeeper or attack the opponent at the moment of reception of the ball entering into physical contact with him; – players should perform passes and shots on goal exactly with the same leg which made the first touch in certain situation; – players should perform passes and shot on goal after the first touch as quick as possible; – players from the attacking team should try to finish the attack quickly with a shot on goal;

Task № 1 continuation

Task description	Requirements for quality of the task execution
Players from the attacking team try to deliver the ball to the attacking zone using passes as quick as possible and shoot on goal from this zone. All players from the attacking team should pass the ball and shoot on goal **necessarily with the second touch performed without a delay after the first with the same leg which made the first,** except finishing off into the net. If player performs the second touch (pass or shot on goal) with a delay in time after the first or with another leg, the ball is transferred to the opponent's team. Number of passes by attacking players in the defending zone before sending the ball across the midline is no more than three. Players from the defending team try to prevent players from the attacking team from delivering the ball to the attacking zone and shooting on goal, situating in the opponent's team defending zone during putting the ball into play. Corners are not awarded. **Offsides are given.** Goal scored at the rebound counts as two. Play time in one repeat – 5 minutes	– attacking player should try to get into such positions that the player possessing the ball always would have an opportunity to provide a pass with the second touch, following after the first without a delay; – players should use every opportunity to finish off the ball into the net; – during the shots on goal performance players should press for sending the ball into the area of the goal unprotected by the goalkeeper

Task № 2	
Task description	Requirements for quality of the task execution
Six attacking players on two defending players play in two zones providing passing space using passes with the second touch performed after the first without a delay. Pitch size: 15 meters wide, 30 meters long. There are three zones marked on the pitch: attacking and defending 13 meters long each, and the middle 4 meters long. «Areas of the ball reception» are marked in attacking and defending zones no further than 7 meters from the middle zone. Three attacking and one defending player act in each «area of the ball reception» all the time. Players are prohibited from moving from zone to zone. 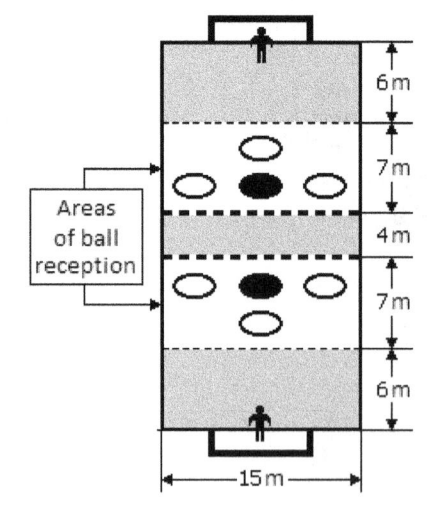	– goalkeepers should put the ball into play without a delay; – defending players should intercept the ball during the pass performance or attack the opponent at the moment of reception of the ball entering into physical contact with him; – players should perform passes and shots on goal exactly with the same leg which made the first touch in certain situation; – players should perform passes and shot on goal after the first touch as quick as possible; – attacking players should try to get into such positions that the player possessing the ball would always have an ability to perform a pass with the second touch following after the first without a delay;

SOCCER. Gaming drills with the contiguous goals for play technique training

Task № 2 continuation

Task description	Requirements for quality of the task execution
On a signal goalkeepers put the ball into play to their team defending zone after catching it or when it is over the goal-line and touchlines. Three attacking players try to pass the ball as quick as possible to partners in «the area of ball reception» in the attacking zone for shooting on goal from this area of the pitch. All attacking players should pass the ball and shoot on goal **necessarily with the second touch, performed after the first without a delay with the same leg the first touch was performed.** Players are permitted to finish off the ball into the net in the goal-area. Goal scored in such manner counts as two. One defending player tries to prevent attacking players from delivering the ball to the attacking zone, and another – to shoot on goal. Corners are not awarded. Offsides are not given. The task for six attacking players is to score maximum number of goals in definite time. Variant: six attacking players on three defending players play. Two defending players act in «areas of ball reception» (one in the defending zone, and another – in the attacking) all the time, and third defending player – in the midfield zone	– attacking players situating in different zones should act simultaneously while trying to deliver the ball from the defending zone to the attacking; – after receiving the ball from the defending zone attacking players should try to finish attack with the shot on goal quickly; – players should try to use every opportunity to finish off the ball into the net; – during the shots on goal performance players should press for sending the ball into the area of the goal unprotected by the goalkeeper

Section 3. Drills suggesting passing the space using passes on medium and long distance

Task № 1	
Task description	Requirements for quality of the task execution
Two on two play with two «neutral» players acting for the attacking team all the time providing passing the space using passes on medium and long distance. Pitch size: 20 meters wide, 50 meters long. There are three zones marked on the pitch: attacking and defending 15 meters long each, and the middle 20 meters long. «Areas of ball reception» are marked in attacking and defending zones no further than 10 meters from the middle zone of the pitch. One player from each team acts in «area of ball reception» in the defending zone all the time, and another – in «area of ball reception» in the attacking zone. One «neutral» player acts in «area of ball reception» in one team defending zone all the time, and another – in «area of ball reception» in another team defending zone. Players are prohibited from moving from zone to zone. On a signal goalkeepers put the ball into play to «area of ball reception» in their team defending zone after catching it or when it is over the goal-line and touchlines. Players from the attacking team try to pass the ball to partners in «area of ball reception» in attacking zone as quick as possible for shooting on goal from this area of the pitch.	– goalkeepers should put the ball into play without a delay; – defending players should intercept the ball during the pass performance or attack the opponent at the moment of reception of the ball entering into physical contact with him; – attacking players acting in one zone should pass the ball to each other timely and precisely, providing partner with the time for performance of pass to the opposite zone; – defending players should attack a player who has possessed the ball as quickly as possible, forcing him to act in conditions of time and space deficit; – players should operate with the ball quickly;

SOCCER. Gaming drills with the contiguous goals for play technique training

Task № 1 continuation

Task description	Requirements for quality of the task execution
(Diagram: field with dimensions 20m wide; top zone 15m with attacker and "Area of ball reception" marked 10m; middle shaded zone 20m; bottom zone with "Area of ball reception" 15m and 10m, attacker at bottom) Players from the attacking team acting in the attacking team are prohibited from playing in one and two touches during ball reception from the defending zone. They are permitted to finish off the ball into the net in the goal-area. Goal scored in such manner counts as two. Corners are not awarded. Offsides are not given. Play time in one repeat – 10 minutes. **Variant:** trajectories of passes to the attacking zone and the length of the middle zone are varied	– attacking players located in different zones should act simultaneously in attempts to deliver the ball from zone to zone; – players should take possession of the ball sent from the defending zone firmly in any case; – attacking players receiving the ball from the defending zone should try to finish the attack with shot on goal quickly; – players should shoot on goal from any, even most inconvenient, positions; – players should press for every opportunity to finish off the ball into the net; – during the shots on goal performance players should press for sending the ball into the area of the goal unprotected by the goalkeeper

Task № 2	
Task description	Requirements for quality of the task execution
Six attacking players on two defending players play in two zones providing passing the space using passes on medium and long distance. Pitch size: 20 meters wide, 50 meters long. There are three zones marked on the pitch: attacking and defending 15 meters long each, and the middle 20 meters long. «Areas of ball reception» are marked in attacking and defending zones no further than 10 meters from the middle zone. Three attacking players and one defending act in each «area of ball reception» all the time. Players are prohibited from moving from zone to zone. Goalkeepers put the ball into play to «area of ball reception» in their team defending zone after catching it or when it is over the goal-line and touchlines. Three attacking players try to pass the ball as quick as possible to «area of ball reception» in the attacking zone on a **mounted trajectory** necessarily so that partner can perform a pass with the head for shooting on goal from this area of the pitch. Number of passes by these players to each other before sending it to the attacking zone is no more than two. Number of passes by attacking players acting in the attacking zone to each other before shooting on goal is no more than two.	– goalkeepers should put the ball into play without a delay; – defending players should intercept the ball during the pass performance or attack the opponent at the moment of reception of the ball entering into physical contact with him; – attacking players acting in the defending zone should pass the ball to each other timely and precisely, providing partner with the time for performance of pass to the opposite zone; – defending players should attack a player who has possessed the ball as quickly as possible, forcing him to act in conditions of time and space deficit; – attacking players should pass the ball to partners in the attacking zone precisely and with a mounted trajectory;

SOCCER. Gaming drills with the contiguous goals for play technique training

Task № 2 continuation

Task description	Requirements for quality of the task execution
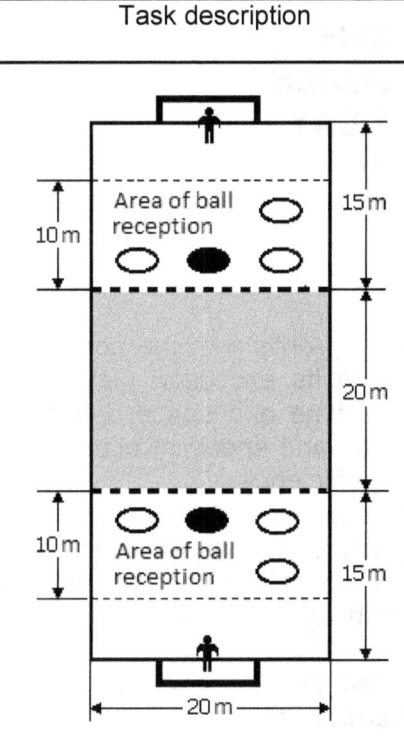 Players are permitted to finish off the ball into the net in the goal-area. Goal scored in such manner counts as two. One of defending players tries to prevent attacking players from passing the ball to the attacking zone, and another – to shoot on goal. The task for six attacking players is to score as much goals as possible in definite time. Offsides are not given. **Variant:** length of the middle zone is varied	– attacking players located in different zones should act simultaneously in attempts to deliver the ball from zone to zone; – attacking players should try to win the ball sent from the defending zone with the head; – attacking players receiving the ball from the defending zone should try to finish the attack with shot on goal quickly; – players should shoot on goal from any, even most inconvenient, positions; – players should press for every opportunity to finish off the ball into the net; – during the shots on goal performance players should press for sending the ball into the area of the goal unprotected by the goalkeeper

CHAPTER V.
THE FEATURES OF GAMING DRILLS BUILD-UP WITH THE CONTIGUOUS GOALS IN THE COURSE OF PLAY TECHNIQUE TRAINING OF YOUNG PLAYERS

Training impact of gaming drills with the contiguous goals is based on that during its execution players are forced to act in conditions of time and space deficit and show definite level in precision and speed of actions with the ball and football «working efficiency».

Concerning young footballers it bears mentioning that the main limiting factor of precise and quick performance of actions with the ball by them is deficient level of ball possession technique and development of necessary physical qualities and functional capabilities. For example, the age conditioned lack of physical qualities limits capability of quality performance of drills suggesting passes on long distance.

Hence requirements for demonstration of precision and speed of actions with the ball, physical qualities and functional capabilities in gaming drills with the contiguous goals should correspond with technical and motive capabilities of young footballers. This may be achieved with assortment of drills and variation of conditions of their performance.

If players are unable to cope with performance of attacking actions with the ball in principle, it is necessary to ease for some time requirements for precision and speed of movements, for example to expand the size of playing ground and zones of players actions, ease restrictions on performance by players some actions with the ball, change objectives for players.

Physical exertion coming on players during performance of gaming drills with the contiguous goals can be varied, for example with change of intensity and duration of drills performance, duration of rest pauses, number of drill repeats, reduction of playing ground size and increase of number of players participating in drill.

While using gaming drills with the contiguous goals in training of young footballers the crucial point is finding of optimal for players of different age goal size.

For training of right habits of shots on goal technique for in-field players and «the goal sense» for young goalkeepers from the first steps in football, in different age groups it is ought to employ goal that:

– correspond with footballers technical, physical and anthropometric capabilities in size;

– should be with «football proportion» in the context of correspondence of its width and height as 3:1 regardless of.

Specifically, using handball goal that often occurs on practice in youth football leads to disruption of structure in attacking and consequently defending actions of in-field players, reinforcement of wrong technical skills of goalkeepers.

Optimal goal sizes for footballers of different age groups are following:

– 7-8-9 years old – 4,5 meters wide and 1,5 meters high;

– 10-11-12 years old – 6 meters wide and 2 meters high;

– 13 years old and older – standard size.

CONCLUSION

Gaming drills with the contiguous goals are one of the kind of drills with variative beginning and finishing of players actions with the ball.

The main method of its organization is carrying out of game episodes on the small area of the pitch with two goals of standard size protected by goalkeepers, with limited number of players in teams and their ultimate commitment, with definite restrictions on performance of some actions and objectives for footballers.

Gaming drills with the contiguous goals allow players of high qualification to improve technical skills in performance of attacking and defending actions, and young footballers – to master technique of these actions.

Using different methodical techniques during construction of these drills allows creating for players conditions for training of wide range of individual and group tactical actions.

In gaming drills with the contiguous goals intensity of footballers' actions can be regulated well definitely, allowing working on building-up of players special working efficiency intentionally.

In work with footballers of younger and teen age during organization of gaming drills with the contiguous goals account must be taken of that requirements for precision and speed of actions with the ball should correspond with technical and motive capabilities of definite players.

It determines necessity for variation of drills conditions in the context of time and space for actions with the ball, demonstration of definite level of physical and functional capabilities.

Practice of using gaming drills with the contiguous goals for play technique training in teams of high qualification (Russian Premier league) and while training of young footballers shows its high efficiency. It is subject to technical skills of performance by players both attacking and defending actions in different zones of the pitch.

High efficiency of these drills is based on that specialized conditions are provided in it in the context of requirements for demonstration by footballers of precision and speed of actions with the ball in different episodes of competitive games and every player is provided with possibility to perform a large number of repeats of one or another actions with the ball in these conditions.

Goalkeepers participating in gaming drills with the contiguous goals have the possibility to train in the most favorable conditions for a long time to develop reactions of anticipation of play situation process and the moment, sped and direction of sending the ball towards the goal in connection with player movements. It allows them to upgrade proficiency of catching and blocking balls promptly, particularly after shots on goal from close distance.

BIBLIOGRAPHY

Бесков К.И. Игровой метод в действии / Футбол: ежегодник 1981. – М.: Физкультура и спорт, 1981. – С. 9-16.

Бишопс К., Герардс Х.-В. Единоборство в футболе. – М.: Терра-Спорт, 2003. – 167 с.

Варюшин В.В. Игровые упражнения в тренировке взаимодействия футболистов: метод. разработки для слушателей ВШТ, факультета повышения квалификации и студентов ГЦОЛИФКа / В.В. Варюшин. – М., ГЦОЛИФК, 1989. – 77 с.

Герасименко А.П. Изучение игровых ситуаций, отражающих связь с игровой деятельностью футболиста / А.П. Герасименко, А.И. Кашигин, В.Д. Князев // В книге: Вопросы управления подготовкой юных спортсменов. – Волгоград, 1979. – С. 25-28.

Голомазов С., Чирва Б. «Игра на сближенных воротах» как средство повышения результативности игры в штрафной площади // Теория и практика футбола. – 2000. – № 3. – С. 19-26.

Голомазов С., Чирва Б. Упражнения игрового характера для совершенствования техники игры головой в штрафной площади / С. Голомазов, Б. Чирва // Теория и практика футбола. – 2002. – № 4. – С. 29-33.

Голомазов С.В., Чирва Б.Г. Теория и методика футбола. Том 1. Техника игры. – М.: СпортАкадемПресс, 2008. – 475 с.

Ковтученко А.И. Некоторые статистические закономерности в футболе / А.И. Ковтученко // Теория и практика физической культуры. – 1975. – № 1. – С. 20-22.

Лисенчук Г.А., Лоос В.Г., Догадайло В.Г. Современные тактические концепции /В книге: Тактика футбола. – Киев, Республиканский научно-методический кабинет Министерства Украины по делам молодежи и спорта, 1991. – С. 17-26.

Никитин Д.В. Оптимизация планирования специализированных упражнений в учебно-тренировочном процессе высококвалифицированных футболистов: автореф. дис. ... канд. пед. наук / Д.В. Никитин; ВГАФК. – Волгоград, 1998. – 23 с.

Петухов А.В. Формирование основ индивидуального технико-тактического мастерства юных футболистов. – М.: Советский спорт, 2006. – 232 с.

Плон Б. 40 игр и игровых упражнений в футбольной тренировке. – М.: Терра-Спорт, 1998. – 47 с.

Плон Б. Новая школа в футбольной тренировке / Б. Плон. – М.: Терра-Спорт, 2003. – 240 с.

Хеддерготт К.-Х. Упражнения на ограниченной площадке / В книге: Новая футбольная школа // К.-Х. Хеддерготт. – М.: Физкультура и спорт, 1976. – С. 144-150.

Цирик Б.Я. Игровые упражнения в тренировке футболистов / Б.Я. Цирик. – М.: Физкультура и спорт, 1961. – 103 с.

Цубан Ю.В. Моделирование игровых упражнений в системе подготовки футболистов на этапе спортивного совершенствования: автореф. дис. ... канд. пед. наук / Ю.В. Цубан; ВНИИФК. – М., 2003. – 24 с.

Чесно Ж.-Л. Футбол. Обучение базовой технике (пер. с французского) / Ж.-Л. Чесно, Ж. Дюрэ. – М.: СпортАкадемПресс, 2002. – 170 с.

Чирва Б. Методология построения упражнений для совершенствования «техники эпизодов игры» в зоне атаки // Теория и практика футбола. – 2001. – № 3. – С. 34-36.

Чирва Б., Голомазов С. Футбол. Игровые упражнения при сближенных воротах для обучения игре в штрафной площади футболистов 11-15 лет: метод. разработки для тренеров. Выпуск 22 / Б. Чирва, С. Голомазов. – М., РГУФК, 2004. – 35 с.

Чирва Б.Г. Игровые упражнения для отработки способов доставки мяча в штрафную площадь // Футбол-Профи. – Донецк (Украина). – август 2005 г. – С. 22-25.

Чирва Б.Г. Организация игровых упражнений при сближенных воротах для тренировки юными футболистами атакующих действий в штрафной площади / Б.Г. Чирва // Физическая культура: воспитание, образование, тренировка. – 2006. – № 4. – С. 32-33.

Чирва Б.Г. Футбол. Методика совершенствования «техники эпизодов игры»: учеб. пособие для студентов высших учебных заведений / Б.Г. Чирва. – М.: ТВТ Дивизион, 2006. – 112 с.

Чирва Б.Г. Футбол. Игровые упражнения при сближенных воротах для тренировки техники игры: учебн. пособие / Б.Г. Чирва. – М.: ТВТ Дивизион, 2008. – 120 с.

Чирва Б. Варианты игровых упражнений при сближенных воротах для тренировки доставки мяча в штрафную площадь из области, находящейся в зоне атаки напротив штрафной площади / Б. Чирва // Теория и практика футбола. – 2009. – № 1. – С. 30-35.

Чирва Б.Г. Футбол. Концепция технической и тактической подготовки футболистов. – 2-е изд., перераб. и доп. – М.: ТВТ Дивизион, 2015. – 352 с.

Better Soccer More Enioyment. «4 v 4». – Zeist (The Netherlands), KNVB, 2006. – 134 p.

Coerver W., Galustian A. Score: soccer tactics techniques for a Better Offense. – Sterling Publishing Co, Ins. New York, 1995. – 190 p.

Michels R. Teambuilding – the road to success. – The Netherlands, Leeuwarden, 2001. – 296 p.

Chirva Boris Grigorievich

Ph.D. in Physical Education, obtains coaching license grade «A», leading Russian soccer strategist. He was born in 1959 and lives in Moscow, Russia.

Previously he was a player of professional soccer teams in First and Second division of USSR championship.

After ending his soccer career he worked as a youth teams coach for eight years and cultivated a player – champion of USSR Under-16-17.

In 1992-93 he was educating in Russian Higher coaching school. Thereafter he began to work on scientific-methods. He passed Ph. D. defense on young players cultivation in 1997, and defended doctoral dissertation about «Basic and professional technical and tactical training of players» in 2008.

During 1999-2013 he was scientific consultant on training methods and worked as a coach in Russian Premier-league clubs. From 2006 till 2008 he worked in Abramovich's National academy of soccer foundation, where were engaged in professional development of Russian youth coaches and methodological support of youth soccer schools and academies.

At the moment he is an educator in Russian coaching license courses in grades «B», «A» and «PRO».

Currently he has published 170 scientific-methods works on various issues of professional and young players training, including 24 monographs, and also he is an author of two training films about players training.

The main direction of his creative activity today is the continuation of work on creation of «Theory and methods of world soccer» in 5 sections: training of soccer technique, preparation and play of professional teams, preparation and play of goalkeepers, soccer strategy and tactic, cultivation of young players.

www.ingramcontent.com/pod-product-compliance
Lightning Source LLC
Chambersburg PA
CBHW071519040426
42444CB00008B/1722